The METHUEN book
of Theatre
Verse

£15.99

**Please return this book
on or before the last**

for

D1492470

L32

THE METHUEN
BOOK OF THEATRE VERSE

The Methuen Book of

THEATRE VERSE

COMPILED BY

Jonathan Field

EDITED BY

Moira Field

Methuen Drama

This book first published in Great Britain
in 1991 by Methuen Drama,
Michelin House, 81 Fulham Road, London sw3 6rb.

A CIP catalogue record for this book
is available from the British Library.
ISBN 0 413 66120 2

Printed in England
by Clays Ltd, St Ives plc
Photoset by Rowland Phototypesetting Ltd
Bury St Edmunds, Suffolk

Contents

Illustrations

ILLUSTRATIONS

The world's a stage – as Shakespeare said one day;
The stage a world – was what he meant to say.

OLIVER WENDELL HOLMES (1858)

Introduction

This collection began to be assembled by my husband, Jonathan Field, over fifty years ago, as a kind of scrapbook of theatre history, both prose and verse, into which he gathered up anything he found that was curious, comical, moving or penetrating – in short, anything revealing of the nature of theatre. But it remained a scrapbook, without the cohesion and unity needed for a true anthology. He felt it lacked the stuff of drama itself, the total experience which comes only when what the author maps out and the actor fulfils is received by the spectator. And he came to the conclusion that to evoke the essence of this experience, rather than simply describe it, he must use verse alone, because verse is itself the very language of experience. So his anthology became a book of verse, and it falls to me to introduce it.

The collection, though wide in scope in that it looks at the theatrical experience from many angles, is confined to the western theatre tradition and, within that, concerns itself largely with the British stage. It is divided into eight sections, each purporting to deal with a particular aspect of theatre. I say purporting to deal, because in fact such neat divisions do not exist in the theatre any more than in life. Within the sections the poems follow a natural course of ideas, occasionally chronological, but more often according to theme or mood.

First, we dwell on the place where it all happens, the stage, which can be anywhere, indoors or out, but most notably in the playhouse proper, whether converted barn or architectural monument. Then we come to the audience – us – without whom there is no drama, since it is all for us and about us. Next, the playwrights, reflecting, and reflecting on, the pre-occupations of their different ages, for 'there is a mode in plays as well as clothes,' as Dryden puts it. Then come the actors, giving flesh and blood to the dramatist's thought, mediating between him and the audience, followed by the parts which actors play and on which poets build fantasies. Backstage is next, the secret infrastructure, the nuts and bolts holding the magic together. After that, the theatrical way of life, the business: success and failure, the sweat under the glamour, fame and its sometimes bitter aftermath. Last, the all-pervasive metaphor, the theatre of the world:

> 'Built with star-galleries of high ascent,
> In which Jehove doth as spectator sit.'

This is a book of theatre verse, not theatre history, though much of that is reflected in it. It is for reading and relish, and the few short notes are there simply to touch in a background that may have become a little blurred with time. For all writers are fully modern at the time of writing and, though the context may have changed, the import of what they have to say can still sound loud and clear to us, whatever the date at the foot of the poem. To let their voices come through un-impeded, we have sometimes adjusted their spelling and punctuation to our own conventions.

Quite a number of the earlier pieces were untitled by their authors, and to some of these, as well as to extracts taken from longer poems, we have given what may be called signpost headings. These are printed between single inverted commas to distinguish them from original titles. Another change made in some of the longer pieces of verse has been to divide up continuous passages into smaller sections. These are chiefly prologues and epilogues of plays, and would have been sim-ilarly broken up in performance by the players delivering them. We have done for the eye what they did for the ear.

Of course the collection is not comprehensive of every single feature of the dramatic experience. For one thing, we could not include what has not been written – poets have not always been considerate enough to celebrate the greatest actors or explore the most intriguing topics. Perhaps it is as well, or we should have needed not eight sections but eight volumes. As it is, we have not had room for all that we should have liked to include. But most experiences in the playhouse, from unlocking the stage door to ringing down the final curtain, have found a place here, and it should be no surprise that the range of subject matter is matched by variety of poetic quality. After all, if we do not expect Dryden to operate the ghost-trap, neither should we look for the style of Byron from the man who works the limes. But they all have their special insights, and together they demonstrate that 'drama is the realm where we can look at all human experience for good or ill without the hampering of restriction, prejudice or censure if we so choose. This is the place in life where the nobodies feature as advantageously as the somebodies. Only in the theatre and the doctor's consulting room do people matter before they are judged.' These are Jonathan's words. He himself would have quoted Shaw, who defined the theatre as: 'A factory of thought, a prompter of conscience, an elucidator of social conduct, an armory against despair and dulness, and a Temple of the Ascent of Man.'

This has always been Jonathan's book, and still is, but he died just when it was about to be published, and, like the understudy who suddenly has to go on for the part, I found myself unexpectedly out there with the curtain going inexorably up. But I have been well supported. I am indebted to Mary O'Donovan, Briar Silich and all the others at Methuen who have taken so much trouble to see the book through to its completion, and I owe particular thanks to Michael Earley for his encouragement and imaginative involvement in the anthology, with all the work and effort that has entailed. I am very grateful, too, to Mandy Little for her sensitive handling of negotiations during my husband's illness, and for her continuing support. Family and friends have given me space, understanding, and help on demand. My thanks go especially to Elizabeth Orna for her generous practical help and counsel; to Jay Reddaway and Andolie Luck for giving me boundless hospitality and a quiet London haven to work from; and above all to Andrew Treagus for all he meant to Jonathan and the confidence he gave to me.

Moira Field
September 1991

THE PLAYHOUSE

The players on the Bankside,
The round Globe and the Swan,
Will teach you idle tricks of love,
But the Bull will play the man.

WILLIAM TURNER (1612)

This is a Theatre

This is a theatre, a place
Of modern art and ancient grace.
(No, child, there is no knob to turn:
I see you have a lot to learn.)
The lights go low, the band begins –
Yes, those are real violins.
The curtain rises – that's a joy
You never knew before, poor boy –
And there are waiting in the wings
Not photographs, but living things;
Yes, all the people in the play
Are only fifty feet away.
The golden girl you seem to like
Is not a myth before a mike:
She's flesh and blood, and well aware
That you, more flesh and blood, are there:
And if you laugh, or weep, or thrill,
She'll know – and she'll do better still.
Your little life, I know, has been
Spent with the shadows on the screen:
Old-fashioned stuff – quite good, it's true;
But this is real – this is NEW.

A P HERBERT (c 1950)

'Theatre in the Open Air'

After a fanfare, the crying of the play,
The Castle of Perseverance

Glorious God! In all degrees, most of might,
    That heaven and earth made of nought, both sea and
        land,
The angels in heaven, him to serve bright,
    And mankind in middle-earth, that he made with his
        hand,
And Our Lovely Lady, that lantern is of light –
    Save our liege lord, the King, the leader of this land,
And all nobles of this realm, and counsel them aright,
    And all the good commons of this town that before us
        stand
                    In this place! . . .

Grace if God will grant us, of his mickle might,
    These pieces in properties we purpose us to play
This day seven-night, before you in sight
    At N _____ on the green, in royal array.
Haste ye then thitherward, sirs, if you please, every wight!
    All good neighbours, full specially we you pray!
And look that ye be there betimes, ready, with heart light,
    For we shall be onward ere it be noon-day.
                    Dear friends,
                We thank you for all good dalliance,
                And for all your special solace,
                And pray you be of good countenance
                    To our lives' ends.

On our lives, we love you, thus taking our leave.
    Ye manly men of this town, thus Christ save you all!
May he maintain your mirths and keep you from grief
    That was born of Mary mild in an ox stall.
Now mercy be on all you people, and well may ye achieve!
    All our faithful friends, thus fair you befall!

Yea, and welcome be ye when ye come, our prowess to
    prove,
  And worthy and worshipful in bower and in hall,
             And in every place.
       Farewell, fair friends,
       That kindly will list and attend.
       Christ keep you from fiends!
          Trump up! And let us pace!

ANON (*c* 1425)

Early travelling players set up their staging out of doors on a
convenient site at each town or village where they played, sending
proclamation of their coming some days ahead by an announce-
ment, known as the Banns, delivered by two flag-bearers and
heralded by trumpets – a vocal playbill.

'Play in the Great Hall'

Prologue to *Fulgens and Lucrece*, played at a Banquet given
by Cardinal Morton, Archbishop of Canterbury, at
Lambeth Palace

(*A enters, as though one of the guests.*)

A   Ah! for God's will,
      What mean ye, sirs, to stand so still?
      Have not ye eaten and your fill,
        And paid nothing therefore?
      I wis, sirs, thus dare I say,
      He that shall for the shot pay
      Vouchsafeth that ye largely assay
        Such meat as he hath in store.

I trow your dishes be not bare,
Nor yet ye do the wine spare;
Therefore be merry as ye fare!
  Ye are welcome each one
Unto this house without faining.
But I marvel much of one thing,
That after this merry drinking
  And good recreation

There are no words among this press,
Non sunt loquelae neque sermones,
But as it were men in sadness.
  Here ye stand musing
Whereabout I cannot tell:
Here should be some revel
Or some else pretty damsel
  For to dance and spring!

Tell me, what call't, is it not so?
I am sure here shall be somewhat ado,
And I wis I will know it ere I go
  Without I be driven hence.

(*Enter B, in similar guise, and speaks.*)

B Nay nay, hardily, man, I undertake
  No man will such mastries make,
  An it were but for the manner sake,
    Thou mayest tarry by licence

  Among other men and see the play,
  I warrant no man will say thee nay.
A I think it well, even as ye say,
    That no man will me grieve.
  But I pray you tell me that again,
  Shall here be a play?
B   Yea, for certain.

A   By my troth, thereof am I glad and fain,
      An ye will me believe;

Of all the world I love such sport,
It doth me so much pleasure and comfort,
And that causeth me ever to resort
      Where such thing is to do.
I trow your own self be one
Of them that shall play.

B   Nay, I am none;
I trow thou speakest in derision
      To liken me thereto.

A   Nay, I mock not, wot ye well,
For I thought verily by your apparel
That ye had been a player.
B   Nay, never a dell.

A   Then I cry you mercy,
I was to blame. Lo therefore I say
There is so much nice array
Amongst these gallants nowaday,
      That a man shall not lightly

Know a player from another man.
But now to the purpose where I began,
I see well here shall be a play than.

B   Yea, that there shall, doubtless,
And I trow ye shall like it well.

A   It seemeth then that ye can tell
Somewhat of the matter.

B   Yea, I am of counsel,
One told me all the process.

A   And I pray you what shall it be?
B   By my faith, as it was told me
         More than once or twice,
     As far as I can bear it away,
     All the substance of their play
         Shall proceed this wise.

HENRY MEDWALL (*c* 1497)

Household plays were often presented during banquets in the halls of palaces or great houses, especially at Christmas time. There was some interplay between actors and guests, as is suggested here by the fact that two of the players pretend at first to be onlookers.

'This Wooden O'

Prologue to *King Henry the Fifth*

O for a Muse of fire, that would ascend
The brightest heaven of invention,
A kingdom for a stage, princes to act,
And monarchs to behold the swelling scene!
Then should the warlike Harry, like himself,
Assume the port of Mars; and at his heels,
Leash'd in like hounds, should famine, sword, and fire,
Crouch for employment. But pardon, gentles all,
The flat unraised spirits that hath dar'd
On this unworthy scaffold to bring forth
So great an object. Can this cockpit hold
The vasty fields of France? Or may we cram
Within this wooden O the very casques
That did affright the air at Agincourt?
O, pardon! since a crooked figure may
Attest in little place a million;
And let us, ciphers to this great accompt,
On your imaginary forces work.
Suppose within the girdle of these walls

Are now confin'd two mighty monarchies,
Whose high upreared and abutting fronts
The perilous narrow ocean parts asunder.
Piece out our imperfections with your thoughts:
Into a thousand parts divide one man,
And make imaginary puissance;
Think, when we talk of horses, that you see them
Printing their proud hoofs i' th' receiving earth;
For 'tis your thoughts that now must deck our kings,
Carry them here and there, jumping o'er times,
Turning th' accomplishment of many years
Into an hour-glass; for the which supply,
Admit me Chorus to this history;
Who, prologue-like, your humble patience pray
Gently to hear, kindly to judge, our play.

WILLIAM SHAKESPEARE (c 1599)

A Sonnet upon the Pitiful Burning of the Globe Playhouse in London

A Broadsheet Ballad

Now sit thee down, Melpomene,
Wrapped in a sea-coal robe,
And tell the doleful tragedy
That late was played at Globe;
For no man that can sing and say
Was scared on St Peter's Day.
Oh sorrow, pitiful sorrow, and yet all this is true.

All you that please to understand,
Come listen to my story;
To see Death with his raking brand
'Mongst such an auditory;
Regarding neither Cardinal's might,
Nor yet the rugged face of Henry the eight.
Oh sorrow, pitiful sorrow, and yet all this is true.

9

This fearful fire began above,
A wonder strange and true,
And to the stage-house did remove,
As round as tailor's clew;
And burnt down both beam and snag,
And did not spare the silken flag.
Oh sorrow, pitiful sorrow, and yet all this is true.

Out run the knights, out run the lords,
And there was great ado;
Some lost their hats and some their swords,
Then out run Burbage too;
The reprobates, though drunk on Monday,
Prayed for the fool and Henry Condye.
Oh sorrow, pitiful sorrow, and yet all this is true.

The periwigs and drum-heads fry,
Like to a butter firkin;
A woeful burning did betide
To many a good buff jerkin.
Then with swollen eyes, like drunken Flemings,
Distressed stood old stuttering Hemings.
Oh sorrow, pitiful sorrow, and yet all this is true.

No shower his rain did there down force,
In all that sunshine weather,
To save that great renowned house,
Nor thou, O ale-house, neither.
Had it begun below, *sans doute*,
Their wives for fear had pissed it out.
Oh sorrow, pitiful sorrow, and yet all this is true.

Be warned, you stage strutters all,
Lest you again be catched,
And such a burning do befall
As to them whose house was thatched;
Forbear your whoring, breeding biles,
And lay up that expense for tiles.
Oh sorrow, pitiful sorrow, and yet all this is true.

Go draw you a petition,
And do you not abhor it,
And get, with low submission,
A license to beg for it
In churches, *sans* churchwardens' checks,
In Surrey and in Middlesex.
Oh sorrow, pitiful sorrow, and yet all this is true.

ANON (1613)

The Globe ('this wooden O') was built in 1598–9 by Cuthbert Burbage, brother of the actor Richard Burbage. It was during a performance of *Henry VIII* (subtitled *All is True*) on 29 June 1613 that the thatch over the stage caught fire, probably from the wadding of a gun fired in the course of the action, and the playhouse went up in flames. It was rebuilt with a tiled roof and reopened the following year, flourishing until 1642, when it was closed by the Puritan Parliament with the other London playhouses. Two years later the Burbages' lease of the site ran out and the ground landlord demolished the building.

As gold is better that's in fire tried,
    So is the Bank-side Globe that late was burn'd;
For where before it had a thatched hide,
    Now to a stately theatre 'tis turn'd:
Which is an emblem, that great things are won
By those that dare through greatest dangers run.

JOHN TAYLOR (1614)

'A Brother Prays'

From *The Muse's Looking Glass*

> . . . That the Globe
Wherein (quoth he) reigns a whole world of vice,
Had been consumed: the Phoenix burnt to ashes:
The Fortune whipp'd for a blind whore: Blackfriars,
He wonders how it scaped demolishing
I' th' time of reformation: lastly he wou'd
The Bull might cross the Thames to the Bear Garden,
And there be soundly baited.

THOMAS RANDOLPH (1630)

'Sir Christopher Wren's Plain-Built House'

From the Prologue spoken at the opening of the new King's House in Drury Lane, March 26th 1674

A plain-built house, after so long a stay,
Will send you half unsatisfied away;
When, fallen from your expected pomp, you find
A bare convenience only is designed.
You, who each day can theatres behold,
Like Nero's palace, shining all with gold,
Our mean ungilded stage will scorn, we fear,
And for the homely room disdain the cheer.
Yet now cheap druggets to a mode are grown,
And a plain suit, since we can make but one,
Is better than to be by tarnished gawdry known.
They, who are by your favours wealthy made,
With mighty sums may carry on the trade;
We, broken banquiers, half destroyed by fire,
With our small stock to humble roofs retire;
Pity our loss, while you their pomp admire.

For fame and honour we no longer strive;
We yield in both, and only beg to live;
Unable to support their vast expense,
Who build and treat with such magnificence,
That, like the ambitious monarchs of the age,
They give the law to our provincial stage. . . .

'Twere folly now a stately pile to raise,
To build a playhouse, while you throw down plays;
Whilst scenes, machines, and empty operas reign,
And for the pencil you the pen disdain;
While troops of famished Frenchmen hither drive,
And laugh at those upon whose alms they live:
Old English authors vanish, and give place
To these new conquerors of the Norman race. . . .

Well, please yourselves; but sure 'tis understood,
That French machines have ne'er done England good.
I would not prophesy our house's fate;
But while vain shows and scenes you overrate,
'Tis to be feared —
That, as a fire the former house o'erthrew,
Machines and tempests will destroy the new.

JOHN DRYDEN (1674)

The first Theatre Royal was built off Drury Lane in 1663, but was gutted by fire in 1671. Dryden extols the austerity of the new theatre which replaced it, contrasting it with its rival, the Duke's Theatre in Dorset Garden. A greatly enlarged Drury Lane Theatre was opened in 1794, boasting the security of a fireproof safety curtain; which did not, however, prevent it from being burnt down in 1809. The fourth Drury Lane opened in 1812, and it still stands today.

The Playhouse

Where gentle Thames through stately channels glides,
And England's proud metropolis divides;
A lofty fabric does the sight invade,
And stretches o'er the waves a pompous shade;
Whence sudden shouts the neighbourhood surprise,
And thundering claps and dreadful hissings rise.

Here thrifty Rich hires monarchs by the day,
And keeps his mercenary kings in pay;
With deep-mouthed actors fills the vacant scenes,
And rakes the stews for goddesses and queens:
Here the lewd punk, with crowns and sceptres graced,
Teaches her eyes a more majestic cast;
And hungry monarchs with a numerous train
Of suppliant slaves, like Sancho, starve and reign.

But enter in, my Muse; the stage survey,
And all its pomp and pageantry display;
Trap-doors and pit-falls, form th' unfaithful ground,
And magic walls encompass it around:
On either side maimed temples fill our eyes,
And intermixed with brothel-houses rise;
Disjointed palaces in order stand,
And groves obedient to the mover's hand
O'ershade the stage, and flourish at command.
A stamp makes broken towns and trees entire:
So when Amphion struck the vocal lyre,
He saw the spacious circuit all around,
With crowding woods and rising cities crowned.

But next the tiring-room survey, and see
False titles, and promiscuous quality,
Confus'dly swarm, from heroes and from queens,
To those that swing in clouds and fill machines.
Their various characters they choose with art,
The frowning bully fits the tyrant's part:

Swoll'n cheeks and swaggering belly make an host,
Pale meagre looks and hollow voice a ghost;
From careful brows and heavy downcast eyes,
Dull cits and thick-skulled aldermen arise:
The comic tone, inspired by Congreve, draws
At every word, loud laughter and applause:
The whining dame continues as before,
Her character unchanged, and acts a whore.

Above the rest, the prince with haughty stalks
Magnificent in purple buskins walks:
The royal robes his awful shoulders grace,
Profuse of spangles and of copper-lace:
Officious rascals to his mighty thigh,
Guiltless of blood, th' unpointed weapon tie:
Then the gay glittering diadem put on,
Ponderous with brass, and starred with Bristol-stone.
His royal consort next consults her glass,
And out of twenty boxes culls a face;
The whitening first her ghastly looks besmears,
All pale and wan th' unfinished form appears;
Till on her cheeks the blushing purple glows,
And a false virgin-modesty bestows.
Her ruddy lips the deep vermilion dyes;
Length to her brows the pencil's art supplies,
And with black bending arches shades her eyes.
Well pleased at length the picture she beholds,
And spots it o'er with artificial moulds;
Her countenance complete, the beaux she warms
With looks not hers: and, spite of nature, charms.

Thus artfully their persons they disguise,
Till the last flourish bids the curtain rise.
The prince then enters on the stage in state;
Behind, a guard of candle-snuffers wait:
There swoll'n with empire, terrible and fierce,
He shakes the dome, and tears his lungs with verse:
His subjects tremble; the submissive pit,

Wrapped up in silence and attention, sit;
Till, freed at length, he lays aside the weight
Of public business and affairs of state:
Forgets his pomp, dead to ambitious fires,
And to some peaceful brandy-shop retires;
Where in full gills his anxious thoughts he drowns,
And quaffs away the care that waits on crowns.

The princess next her painted charms displays,
Where every look the pencil's art betrays;
The callow squire at distance feeds his eyes,
And silently for paint and washes dies:
But if the youth behind the scenes retreat,
He sees the blended colours melt with heat,
And all the trickling beauty run in sweat.
The borrowed visage he admires no more,
And nauseates every charm he loved before:
So the famed spear, for double force renowned,
Applied the remedy that gave the wound.

In tedious lists 'twere endless to engage,
And draw at length the rabble of the stage,
Where one for twenty years has given alarms,
And called contending monarchs to their arms;
Another fills a more important post,
And rises every other night a ghost;
Through the cleft stage his mealy face he rears,
Then stalks along, groans thrice, and disappears;
Others, with swords and shields, the soldier's pride,
More than a thousand times have changed their side,
And in a thousand fatal battles died.

Thus several persons several parts perform;
Soft lovers whine, and blustering heroes storm.
The stern exasperated tyrants rage,
Till the kind bowl of poison clears the stage.
Then honours vanish, and distinctions cease;
Then, with reluctance, haughty queens undress.

Heroes no more their fading laurels boast,
And mighty kings in private men are lost.
He, whom such titles swelled, such power made proud,
To whom whole realms and vanquished nations bowed,
Throws off the gaudy plume, the purple train,
And in his own vile tatters stinks again.

Attributed to JOSEPH ADDISON (c 1700)

This peep behind the scenes – almost a play in itself – is based on
Drury Lane in the early 1690s, at that time under the management of
Christopher Rich (d 1714).

'Builder's Triumph – Actor's Bane'

From *The London Theatres*

In Drury's widen'd amphitheatre
In scenes like these, where sound must be conveyed
To the far distant crowd in gallery rows,
Propriety is outraged. Those below
(Plac'd at just distance, in the neighbouring pit)
Behold the Roman traitor steal toward
The couch of sleeping gentle Imogen,
As fearful every step might wake the fair.
Behold him view the chamber, and, at length,
Note on her bosom the 'cinque spotted' mole:
Then, hear him tell his villainous intent,
In tones high rais'd, discordant, and unfit,
To gods assembled in their lofty seats!

Drury, thy vast and tow'ring space has prov'd
The builder's triumph, but the actor's bane.
On thy broad boards, the whistling winds around
Annoy the shiv'ring hero, as he moves
And chatters o'er his lesson, numb'd by cold
Intense, and hurtful to his powers and frame.

Triumph ye dancing and ye dumb-show tribe,
Where the light heel, a stranger to the head,
Hath now brave footing for its mazy rounds.
Ye bulls, ye bears, rejoice! Ye chargers, thrive,
Thrive in your stalls theatric, pamper'd high,
For grand and glittering spectacles to come.

THOMAS BELLAMY (1795)

Prologue

on the Old Winchester Playhouse built over the Old Butchers' Shambles

Whoe'er our stage examines, must excuse
The wondrous shifts of the dramatic Muse;
Then kindly listen, while the prologue rambles
From wit to beef, from Shakespeare to the shambles!

Divided only by one flight of stairs,
The monarch swaggers, and the butcher swears!
Quick the transition when the curtain drops,
From meek Monimia's moans to mutton-chops!
While for Lothario's loss Lavinia cries,
Old women scold, and dealers d–n your eyes!
Here Juliet listens to the gentle lark,
There in harsh chorus hungry bulldogs bark.
Cleavers and scimitars give blow for blow,
And heroes bleed above, and sheep below!
While tragic thunders shake the pit and box,
Rebellows to the roar the staggering ox.
Cow-horns and trumpets mix their martial tones,
Kidneys and kings, mouthing and marrow-bones.
Suet and sighs, blank verse and blood abound,
And form a tragi–comedy around.
With weeping lovers, dying calves complain,
Confusion reigns – chaos is come again!

Hither your steelyards, butchers, bring, to weigh
The pound of flesh, Antonio's bond must pay!
Hither your knives, ye Christians, clad in blue,
Bring to be whetted by the ruthless Jew!

Hard is our lot, who, seldom doomed to eat,
Cast a sheep's-eye on this forbidden meat –
Gaze on sirloins, which, ah! we cannot carve,
And in the midst of legs of mutton – starve!
But would you to our house in crowds repair,
Ye generous captains, and ye blooming fair,
The fate of Tantalus we should not fear,
Nor pine for a repast that is so near.
Monarchs no more would supperless remain,
Nor pregnant queens for cutlets long in vain.

THOMAS WARTON (*c* 1750)

'Half-Rural Sadler's Wells'
From *The Prelude*

                                    . . . Need I fear
To mention by its name, as in degree
Lowest of these, and humblest in attempt,
Though richly graced with honours of its own,
Half-rural Sadler's Wells? Though at that time
Intolerant, as is the way of Youth
Unless itself be pleased, I more than once
Here took my seat, and, maugre frequent fits
Of irksomeness, with ample recompense
Saw Singers, Rope-dancers, Giants and Dwarfs,
Clowns, Conjurers, Posture-masters, Harlequins,
Amid the uproar of the rabblement,
Perform their feats. Nor was it mean delight
To watch crude nature work in untaught minds,
To note the laws and progress of belief;
Though obstinate on this way, yet on that

How willingly we travel, and how far!
To have, for instance, brought upon the scene
The Champion Jack the Giant-killer, Lo!
He dons his Coat of Darkness; on the Stage
Walks, and atchieves his wonders from the eye
Of living mortal safe as is the moon
'Hid in her vacant interlunar cave'.
Delusion bold! and faith must needs be coy;
How is it wrought? His garb is black, the word
INVISIBLE flames forth upon his chest. . . .

                  . . . Life then was new,
The senses easily pleased; the lustres, lights,
The carving and the gilding, paint and glare,
And all the mean upholstery of the place,
Wanted not animation in my sight:
Far less the living Figures on the Stage,
Solemn or gay: whether some beauteous Dame
Advanced in radiance through a deep recess
Of thick–entangled forest, like the Moon
Opening the clouds; or sovereign King, announced
With flourishing Trumpets, came in full–blown State
Of the world's greatness, winding round with Train
Of Courtiers, Banners, and a length of Guards;
Or Captive led in abject weeds, and jingling
His slender manacles; or romping Girl
Bounced, leapt, and paw'd the air; or mumbling Sire
A scare-crow pattern of old Age, patch'd up
Of all the tatters of infirmity,
All loosely put together, hobbled in,
Stumping upon a Cane, with which he smites,
From time to time, the solid boards, and makes them
Prate somewhat loudly of the whereabout
Of one so overloaded with his years.
But what of this! the laugh, the grin, grimace,
And all the antics and buffoonery,
The least of them not lost, were all received
With charitable pleasure. . . .

Pleasure that had been handed down from times
When, at a Country-Playhouse, having caught,
In summer, through the fractur'd wall, a glimpse
Of daylight, at the thought of where I was
I gladden'd more than if I had beheld
Before me some bright cavern of Romance,
Or than we do, when on our beds we lie
At night, in warmth, when rains are beating hard. . . .

WILLIAM WORDSWORTH (1805)

Theatre

The theatre is a world apart,
No matter what they say.
It has a different kind of heart,
A different kind of day.
It tells of things you dare not tell;
Of ages passed away;
Of Heaven, Earth and deepest Hell,
Of work and love and play.
It's all tied up with sex and death,
With comedy and strife;
And the magic of the human past
The theatre brings to life.
In fact as long as men have minds
And hearts that sometimes break,
They'll always leave the mundane street
To see the gods awake . . .

NICHOLAS SMITH (1963)

Drury Lane A-Burning
With apologies to Sir Walter Scott
From *Rejected Addresses*

As Chaos, which, by heavenly doom,
Had slept in everlasting gloom,
Started with terror and surprise
When light first flash'd upon her eyes –
So London's sons in nightcap woke,
In bedgown woke her dames;
For shouts were heard 'mid fire and smoke,
And twice ten hundred voices spoke –
    'The playhouse is in flames!'

And, lo! where Catherine Street extends,
A fiery tail its lustre lends
    To every window-pane;
Blushes each spout in Martlet Court,
And Barbican, moth-eaten fort,
And Covent Garden kennels sport
    A bright ensanguined drain;
Meux's new brewhouse shows the light,
Rowland Hill's chapel, and the height
    Where patent shot they sell;
The Tennis Court, so fair and tall,
Partakes the ray, with Surgeon's Hall,
The ticket-porters' house of call,
Old Bedlam, close by London Wall,
Wright's shrimp and oyster shop withal,
    And Richardson's Hotel.

Nor these alone, but far and wide,
Across red Thames's gleaming tide,
To distant fields, the blaze was borne,
And daisy white and hoary thorn
In borrow'd lustre seem'd to sham
The rose or red Sweet Wil-li-am.

To those who on the hill around
Beheld the flames from Drury's mound,
        As from a lofty altar rise,
It seem'd that nations did conspire
To offer to the god of fire
        Some vast stupendous sacrifice!

The summon'd firemen woke at call,
And hied them to their stations all:
Starting from short and broken snooze,
Each sought his pond'rous hobnail'd shoes,
But first his worsted hosen plied,
Plush breeches next, in crimson dyed,
        His nether bulk embraced;
Then jacket thick, of red or blue,
Whose massy shoulder gave to view
The badge of each respective crew,
        In tin or copper traced.
The engines thunder'd through the street,
Fire-hook, pipe, bucket, all complete,
And torches glared, and clattering feet
        Along the pavement paced. . . .

HORACE SMITH (1812)

After Drury Lane was burnt down in 1809, a competition was held
to find an address to inaugurate the opening of the new theatre,
which took place in 1812. *Rejected Addresses* purported to be a
collection of genuine entries, which were in fact parodies by the
brothers Horace and James Smith. In the rest of the parody of Scott
quoted here, much play is made with the rivalry between different
fire insurance companies, vying with each other to be first at the fire.

'An Edifice Quite New'

Address on the opening of the New Theatre, North Walsham, Norfolk

From former times this maxim just we trace,
Ne'er meet a friend that's old with a new face.
We, in defiance of a rule so true
Presume, this night, to show a face quite new;
But it's a better face; let that our pardon plead,
And grant your smiles, to make this face succeed.
When two years since, on the same spot we met,
In cold clay walls, with roof of thatch ye sat;
Then Richard, Richmond marshall'd their proud ranks
On stage no bigger than a mountebank's;
Then Scotland's tyrant bravely fought his squadron
In space scarce larger than the witches' cauldron;
Here, as we oft portray'd their furious ire,
The eddy winds damp'd our theatric fire.
Look round, my gen'rous friends, and you'll view
Instead of barn, an edifice quite new;
One more deserving of your lib'ral aid,
One where our drama may be best displayed.
On spacious stage our harmless combats fight
And Richard be himself again each night.
But now, my honoured friends, our thanks are due
For years of kind support received from you;
In grateful homage, we this tribute raise
Sprung from your bounty, cheer it with your praise,
And as, in humble barn, you deign'd to meet us
We hope in this our Theatre you'll greet us.
Greet us with plaudits, if you our taste commend,
And be assured to please you is our end.

CAPTAIN SIMPSON, Royal Marines (1828)

The Best Way to Warm a Playhouse

Addressed to those who complained of the coldness of the Salisbury Theatre

The actors of Sarum have made a great pother,
Abused all the town, and abused one another;
'Cause weather's inclemency hindered their houses,
And robbed them of food, for themselves and their spouses,
A fire have provided, the theatre to warm,
Allure the good folks, and secure them from harm.
A wholesomer method the audience might find them
Than thus to be warmed with a fire behind them:
In shoals thither flock, for experience has told,
That a well-crowded playhouse can never be cold.

JOHN BROWNSMITH (1776)

Over the Water

Look always on the Surrey side
    For true dramatic art.
The road is long – the river wide –
    But frequent buses start
From Charing Cross and Gracechurch street,
    (An inexpensive ride);
So, if you want an evening's treat,
    O seek the Surrey side.

I have been there, and still would go,
    As Dr Watts observes;
Although it's not a place, I know,
    For folks with feeble nerves.
Ah me! how many roars I've had –
    How many tears I've dried –
At melodramas, good and bad,
    Upon the Surrey side.

Can I forget those wicked lords,
    Their voices and their calves;
The things they did upon those boards,
    And never did by halves:
The peasant, brave though lowly born,
    Who constantly defied
Those wicked lords with utter scorn,
    Upon the Surrey side?

Can I forget those hearts of oak,
    Those model British tars;
Who crack'd a skull or crack'd a joke,
    Like true transpontine stars;
Who hornpip'd *à la* T. P. Cooke,
    And sang – at least they tried –
Until the pit and gallery shook,
    Upon the Surrey side?

But best of all I recollect
    That maiden in distress –
So unimpeachably correct
    In morals and in dress –
Who, ere the curtain fell, became
    The low–born peasant's bride:
(They nearly always end the same
    Upon the Surrey side).

I gape in Covent Garden's walls.
    I doze in Drury Lane;
I strive in the Lyceum stalls
    To keep awake – in vain.
There's nought in the dramatic way
    That I can quite abide,
Except the pieces that they play
    Upon the Surrey side.

H S LEIGH (1869)

V is Old Vic. And ain't it a vunder
the vay Villiam Shakespeare becomes blood and thunder?

HUMBERT WOLFE (1932)

Theatre

Where stars for ever set, for ever rise,
Traditions crumbling down from age to age,
Their ancient craft the brotherhood still wage
And many a steadfast artist daily plies;
But now the lights are out, the darkened stage
All still and dead and naked – floor to flies;
Ended the show's pretence and mockeries
Of phantom fun and joy, or grief and rage.
  The curtain's rolled away; each rank and tier,
  Whence we beheld the traffic and the strife,
  Yawns tenantless; yet are there mummers here,
  And dramas, unrehearsed, of humble life
  Proceed, albeit never hand applauds,
  The mice, who nightly hop these classic boards.

EDEN PHILLPOTTS (1929)

At the Theatre

The sun was bright when we went in,
  But night and lights were there,
The walls had golden trimming on
  And plush on every chair.

The people talked; the music played,
  Then it grew black as pitch,
Yes, black as closets full of clothes,
  Or caves, I don't know which.

The curtain rolled itself away,
  It went I don't know where,
But, oh, that country just beyond,
  I do wish we lived there!

The mountain peaks more jaggéd rise,
  Grass grows more green than here;
The people there have redder cheeks,
  And clothes more gay and queer.

They laugh and smile, but not the same,
  Exactly, as we do.
And if they ever have to cry
  Their tears are different too –

More shiny, somehow, and more sad,
  You hold your breath to see
If everything will come out right
  And they'll live happily;

If Pierrot will kiss Pierrette
  Beneath an orange moon,
And Harlequin and Columbine
  Outwit old Pantaloon.

You know they will, they always do,
  But still your heart must beat,
And you must pray they will be saved,
  And tremble in your seat.

And then it's over and they bow
  All edged about with light,
The curtain rattles down and shuts
  Them every one from sight.

It's strange to find the afternoon
Still bright outside the door,
And all the people hurrying by
The way they were before!

RACHEL FIELD (1926)

A Theatre Dies
Stockton Empire

Once, on this very floor
Ellen Terry may have stood.
Once, through that very door
may have sounded loud and long
the shattering applause
of a cheering, glittering throng.
Once, on those very stairs
a princess may have waited
for her prince. Now, who cares?
See how old the curtains grow,
see how dull the seats become;
see the gaslights flicker low
then come to life again.
Look, someone's in a golden box,
and listen to a sweet refrain.
There is gaiety and laughter;
there is smoke and senseless noise;
there is excitement, as after
a star has sung her part.
But stop. For these memories
are tugging at my heart.
For the theatre is empty now.
There is no-one here at all.

The theatre is empty now
and though it's hard to say,
this lovely theatre's empty,
this theatre's had its day.
But a theatre is a living thing;
and they just let it die:
a sordid and a piteous death,
and few will wipe an eye.
Yet I do weep, yes weep for you,
for you are worth much more
than to provide foundation
for some cheap department store.

Now the dealers and the auction men,
the curious and the rest
are here to rob you openly
of what you wore the best.
For a pound go the footlights,
another gets the bar.
For a shilling goes the paybox seat
and nothing can mar
this furious spate of buying
'til the last curtain falls
and little men in aprons
start ripping up the stalls.

LES FREEMAN (1960)

AUDIENCES

The slope of faces, from the floor to th' roof,
(As if one master–spring controll'd them all)
Relax'd into a universal grin.

WILLIAM COWPER (1785)

'A Theatrical Feast'

Prologue to George Farquhar's *The Inconstant, or The Way to Win Him*, at Drury Lane

Like hungry guests a sitting audience looks,
Plays are like suppers: poets are the cooks.
The founders you; the table is this place.
The carvers we, the prologue is the grace.
Each act, a course; each scene, a different dish.
Though we're in Lent, I doubt you're still for flesh –
Satire's the sauce, high-seasoned, sharp, and rough:
Kind masques and beaux, I hope you're pepper-proof.
Wit is the wine; but 'tis so scarce the true,
Poets, like vintners, balderdash and brew.

Your surly scenes, where rant and bloodshed join,
Are butcher's meat, a battle's a sirloin.
Your scenes of love, so flowing, soft, and chaste,
Are water-gruel, without salt or taste.
Bawdy's fat venison, which, too stale, can please:
Your rakes love hogoes like your damned French cheese.
Your rarity for the fair guests to gape on
Is your nice squeaker, or Italian capon;
Or your French virgin-pullet, garnished round
And dressed with sauce of some – four hundred pound.

An opera, like an olio, nicks the age;
Farce is the hasty-pudding of the stage.
For when you're treated with indifferent cheer,
Ye can dispense with slender stage-coach fare.
A pastoral's whipped cream; stage-whims, mere trash;
And tragicomedy, half fish, half flesh.
But comedy, that, that's the darling cheer.
This night we hope you'll an Inconstant bear;
Wild fowl is liked in playhouse all the year.

Yet since each mind betrays a different taste,
And every dish scarce pleases every guest,
If ought you relish, do not damn the rest.
This favour craved, up let the music strike:
You're welcome all – now fall to where you like!

PETER MOTTEUX (1702)

We rather think the persons fit for plays,
Are those whose birth and education says
They've every help that should improve mankind,
Yet still live slaves to a vile tainted mind.

COLLEY CIBBER (1704)

'The Intermittent Playgoer'

Fuscus is free, and hath the world at will,
Yet in the course of life that he doth lead,
He's like a horse which turning round a mill,
Doth always in the selfsame circle tread:
First he doth rise at ten and at eleven
He goes to Giles, where he doth eat till one,
Then sees a play till six, and sups at seven,
And after supper, straight to bed is gone.
And there till ten next day he doth remain,
And then he dines, then sees a comedy,
And then he sups, and goes to bed again:
Thus round he runs without variety:
    Save that sometimes he comes not to the play
    But falls into a whore-house by the way.

SIR JOHN DAVIES (c 1590)

'The Choice'

Speak gentlemen, what shall we do today?
Or shall we to the Globe to see a play?
Or visit Shoreditch for a bawdy-house?

SAMUEL ROWLANDS (1600)

Go to your play-house you shall actors have
Your bawd, your gull, your whore, your pander knave,
Go to your bawdy-house, y'ave actors too
As bawds, and whores, and gulls: panders also.
Besides, in either house (if you enquire)
A place there is for men themselves to tire.
    Since th' are so like, to choose there's not a pin
    Whether bawdy-house or play-house you go in.

WILLIAM GODDARD (1615)

For they, he swears, to the theatre would come,
Ere they had din'd, to take up the best room;
There sit on benches, not adorn'd with mats,
And graciously did vail their high-crown'd hats
To ev'ry half-dress'd player, as we still
Through the hangings peep'd to see how the house did fill.

WILLIAM DAVENANT (c 1638)

'The Lady Goes to the Play'

                   . . . Time's lost
Till a play-bill be sever'd from the post
T' inform you what's to play; then comes your coach,
Where numerous light ones, like yourself, approach,
But where's devotion all this while? Asleep,
And for herself sole sentinel may keep.
But now you're seated, and the music sound
For th' actors' entry; pleasures do abound
In ev'ry box; sometimes your eye's on th' stage,
Straight on a lighter object, your loose page,
Or some fantastic gallant, or your groom,
But when this emblem of your life is done,
This piece of witty art, what do you then?
To your sin-shrouding coaches straight again,
You make repair, where you relaters be
Of what your ear did hear, or eye could see.

RICHARD BRATHWAIT (1635)

Today I go to the Blackfriars Playhouse
Sit i' the view, salute all my acquaintance,
Rise up between the acts, let fall my cloak,
Publish a handsome man, and a rich suit
(As that's a special end, why we go thither,
All that pretend, to stand for 't o' the stage).
The ladies ask who's that? For they do come
To see us, love, as we do to see them.

BEN JONSON (1616)

U is for US. They should pay us a salary
for looking like Daumier prints in the gallery.

HUMBERT WOLFE (1932)

Nocturnal Sketch

Even is come; and from the dark Park, hark,
The signal of the setting sun – one gun!
And six is sounding from the chime, prime time
To go and see the Drury-Lane Dane slain, –
Or hear Othello's jealous doubt spout out, –
Or Macbeth raving at that shade-made blade –
Denying to his frantic clutch much touch; –
Or else to see Ducrow with wide stride ride
Four horses as no other man can span;
Or in the small Olympic Pit, sit split
Laughing at Liston, while you quiz his phiz.

THOMAS HOOD (*c* 1825)

The Moan of a Theatre-Manager

Who gets, by hook or crook, from me
Admittance free, though well knows he
That myriads turned away will be?
                    The Deadhead.

Who, while he for his programme pays
The smallest silver coin, inveighs
Against such fraud with eyes ablaze?
                    The Deadhead.

Who to his neighbour spins harangues,
On how he views with grievous pangs
The dust that on our hangings hangs?
                    The Deadhead.

Who, in a voice which rings afar,
Declares, while standing at the bar,
Our drinks most deleterious are?
                    The Deadhead.

Who, aye withholds the claps and cheers
That others give? Who jeers and sneers
At all he sees and all he hears?
                    The Deadhead.

Who loudly, as the drama's plot
Unfolds, declares the tale a lot
Of balderdash and tommy-rot?
                    The Deadhead.

Who dubs the actors boorish hinds?
Who fault with all the scenery finds?
Who with disgust his molars grinds?
                    The Deadhead.

Who spreads dissatisfaction wide
'Mongst those who else with all they spied
Had been extremely satisfied?
                    The Deadhead.

Who runs us down for many a day,
And keeps no end of folks away
That else would for admittance pay?
                    The Deadhead.

Who keeps his reputation still,
For recompensing good with ill
With more than pandemonium's skill?
                    The Deadhead.

Who makes the bankrupt's doleful doom
In all its blackness o'er me loom?
Who'll bring my grey head to the tomb?
                    The Deadhead.

ARTHUR ST JOHN ADCOCK (1903)

The Queue

Standing in a theatre queue
Is an expensive thing to do.
Street entertainers, hat in hand,
Throng to amuse you while you stand;
One man sings, another fiddles,
One recites and asks you riddles.
This man whistles, that man capers
Or makes designs by tearing papers;
Another simply volunteers
To roll his eyes and wag his ears.
                *   *   *
It costs too much to pay them all,
So slip away and buy a stall.

GUY BOAS (1925)

Q is the queue. How enchanting to sit
in a blizzard all day, and then faint in the pit.

HUMBERT WOLFE (1932)

The Theatre
By the Rev G C
From *Rejected Addresses*

'Tis sweet to view, from half-past five to six,
Our long wax-candles, with short cotton wicks,
Touch'd by the lamplighter's Promethean art,
Start into light, and make the lighter start;
To see red Phoebus through the gallery-pane
Tinge with his beam the beams of Drury Lane;
While gradual parties fill our widen'd pit,
And gape, and gaze, and wonder, ere they sit.

At first while vacant seats give choice and ease,
Distant or near, they settle where they please;
But when the multitude contracts the span,
And seats are rare, they settle where they can.
Now the full benches to late-comers doom
No room for standing, miscall'd *standing room*.

Hark! The check-taker moody silence breaks,
And bawling 'Pit full!' gives the check he takes;
Yet onward still the gathering numbers cram,
Contending crowders shout the frequent damn,
And all is bustle, squeeze, row, jabbering, and jam.
See to their desks Apollo's sons repair –
Swift rides the rosin o'er the horse's hair!
In unison their various tones to tune,
Murmurs the hautboy, growls the hoarse bassoon;
In soft vibration sighs the whispering lute,
Tang goes the harpsichord, too-too the flute,
Brays the loud trumpet, squeaks the fiddle sharp,
Winds the French horn, and twangs the tingling harp;
Till, like great Jove, the leader, figuring in,
Attunes to order the chaotic din.

Now all seems hush'd; but no, one fiddle will
Give, half-ashamed, a tiny flourish still.

Foil'd in his crash, the leader of the clan
Reproves with frowns the dilatory man:
Then on his candlestick thrice taps his bow,
Nods a new signal, and away they go.

Perchance, while pit and gallery cry 'Hats off!'
And awed Consumption checks his chided cough,
Some giggling daughter of the Queen of Love
Drops, reft of pin, her play-bill from above;
Like Icarus, while laughing galleries clap,
Soars, ducks, and dives in air the printed scrap;
But, wiser far than he, combustion fears,
And, as it flies, eludes the chandeliers;
Till, sinking gradual, with repeated twirl,
It settles, curling, on a fiddler's curl,
Who from his powder'd pate, the intruder strikes,
And, for mere malice, sticks it on the spikes.

Say, why these Babel strains from Babel tongues?
Who's that calls 'Silence!' with such leathern lungs?
He who, in quest of quiet, 'Silence!' hoots,
Is apt to make the hubbub he imputes.

What various swains our motley walls contain! –
Fashion from Moorfields, honour from Chick Lane;
Bankers from Paper Buildings here resort,
Bankrupts from Golden Square and Riches Court;
From the Haymarket canting rogues in grain,
Gulls from the Poultry, sots from Water Lane;
The Lottery-cormorant, the auction shark,
The full-price master, and the half-price clerk;
Boys who long linger at the gallery-door,
With pence twice five – they want but twopence more;
Till some Samaritan the twopence spares,
And sends them jumping up the gallery-stairs.

Critics we boast who ne'er their malice balk,
But talk their minds – we wish they'd mind their talk;
Big-worded bullies, who by quarrels live –

Who give the lie, and tell the lie they give;
Jews from St Mary Axe, for jobs so wary,
That for old clothes they'd even axe St Mary;
And bucks with pockets empty as their pate,
Lax in their gaiters, laxer in their gait;
Who oft, when we our house lock up, carouse
With tippling tipstaves in a lock-up house. . . .

JAMES SMITH (1812)

'The Rev G C' to whom this lively description is ascribed is the poet George Crabbe. For the circumstances of its writing, see page 23.

'Full House at the Fortune'
A view from the stage

Nay, when you look into my galleries,
How bravely they're trimm'd up, you all shall swear
You're highly pleas'd to see what's set down there:
Storeys of men and women, mix'd together,
Fair ones with foul, like sunshine in wet weather;
Within one square a thousand heads are laid,
So close that all of heads the room seems made;
As many faces there, fill'd with blithe looks
Shew like the promising titles of new books
Writ merrily, the readers being their own eyes,
Which seem to move and to give plaudities;
And here and there, whilst with obsequious ears
Throng'd heaps do listen, a cut-purse thrusts and leers
With hawk's eyes for his prey; I need not shew him;
By a hanging, villainous look yourselves may know him,
The face is drawn so rarely: then, sir, below,
The very floor, as 't were, waves to and fro,
And, like a floating island, seems to move
Upon a sea bound in with shores above.

THOMAS DEKKER and THOMAS MIDDLETON (1611)

'Full House at Covent Garden'

What an overflowing House, methinks I see!
Here, box-keeper, are these my places? No,
Madam Van Bulk has taken all that row;
Then I'll go back – you can't – you can, she fibs,
Keep down your elbows, or you'll break my ribs;
Zounds, how you squeeze! Of what do you think one made is?
Is this your wig? No, it's that there lady's.
Then the side-boxes, what delightful rows!
Peers, poets, nabobs, Jews, and 'prentice beaux.

MILES PETER ANDREWS (1789)

'Something for Everybody'

How is't possible to suffice
So many ears, so many eyes?
Some in wit, some in shows
Take delight, and some in clothes;
Some for mirth they chiefly come,
Some for passion – for both some;
Some for lascivious meetings, that's their arrant;
Some to detract, and ignorance their warrant,
How is't possible to please
Opinion toss'd in such wild seas?
Yet I doubt not, if attention
Seize you above, and apprehension
You below, to take things quickly,
We shall both make you sad and tickle ye.

THOMAS MIDDLETON (1613)

'On Judgement'

One company knowing they judgement lack,
Ground their belief on the next man in black.
Others, on him that makes signs, and is mute,
Some like as he does in the fairest suit,
He as his mistress doth, and she by chance.
Nor wants there those, who as the boy doth dance
Between the acts, will censure the whole play;
Some if the wax-lights be not new that day;
But multitudes there are whose judgement goes
Headlong according to the actors' clothes.

FRANCIS BEAUMONT (1608)

How can you err? Plays are like paintings tried,
You first enquire the hand, and then decide.
Yet judge him not before the curtain draws,
Lest a fair hearing should reverse the cause.

JOHN GAY (1724)

In other things the knowing artist may
Judge better than the people; but a play,
(Made for delight, and for no other use)
If you approve it not, has no excuse.

EDMUND WALLER (1620)

All this may be; the people's voice is odd,
It is, and it is not, the voice of God.

ALEXANDER POPE (1737)

'A Good Laugh'

From the Praeludium for *The Careless Shepherdess*

Why, I would have the fool in every act,
Be 't comedy or tragedy, I've laugh'd
Until I cried again, to see what faces
The rogue will make. O it does me good
To see him hold out 's chin, hang down his hands,
And twirl his bauble. There is ne'er a part
About him but breaks jests. I heard a fellow
Once on this stage cry, *Doodle, Doodle, Dooe*,
Beyond compare; I'd give the other shilling
To see him act the *Changeling* once again.

ANON (*c* 1638)

There still remains, to mortify a wit,
The many-headed Monster of the Pit:
A senseless, worthless, and unhonoured crowd;
Who, to disturb their betters mighty proud,
Clatt'ring their sticks before ten lines are spoke,
Call for the Farce, the Bear, or the Black-joke.
What dear delight to Britons Farce affords!
Ever the taste of mobs, but now of Lords.

ALEXANDER POPE (1737)

Charge of the Late Brigade

From *Spread It Abroad* at the
Saville Theatre

PROGRAMME-
GIRL:

Here they come, here they come,
    The Always Late Brigade!
Clash the cymbal! beat the drum!
What a scrimmage! what a scrum!
Though they may be troublesome,
    They must be obeyed!
Vainly let the mummer mum
    When they're on parade!

CHORUS OF
LATECOMERS:

Bark the shin and bruise the toe!
Knock the knee as in you go!
Jab the elbow in the eye!
Shout the loud apology!
Seek the sixpence! crush the feet!
Block the view and bang the seat!
None shall stop the nightly raid
Of the Always Late Brigade!

PROGRAMME-
GIRL:

Journalists for ever cry
    They should be suppressed!
Managers intend to try
By-and-by-and-by-and-by!
But, while punctuality
    Is a mere request,
Nothing shall effectively
    Speed the coming guest!

CHORUS OF
LATECOMERS:

Graze the ankle! rip the skirt!
Kick the calf and mind you hurt!
When you've got your victim pinned,
Let him have it in the wind!

Settle loudly in your seats!
Beckon for a box of sweets!
Shout for change to be conveyed!
That's the Always Late Brigade!

HERBERT FARJEON (1936)

'Easy Virtue in the Galleries'

Epilogue to *Sir Courtly Nice*

Our galleries too, were finely us'd of late,
Where roosting masques sat cackling for a mate:
They came not to see plays but act their own,
And had throng'd audiences when we had none.
Our plays it was impossible to hear,
The honest country men were forced to swear:
Confound you, give your bawdy prating o'er,
Or zounds, I'll fling you i' the pit, you bawling whore.

JOHN CROWNE (1685)

'The Noise Continues'

Prologue to Southerne's *The Disappointment*

But stay; methinks some vizard-mask I see
Cast out her lure from the mid gallery:
About her all the fluttering sparks are rang'd;
The noise continues, though the scene is chang'd:
Now growling, sputt'ring, wauling, such a clutter!
'Tis just like puss defendant in a gutter. . . .

Last, some there are, who take their first degrees
Of lewdness in our middle galleries:
The doughty bullies enter bloody drunk,
Invade and grubble one another's punk:
They caterwaul and make a dismal rout,
Call sons of whores, and strike, but ne'er lugg-out:
Thus, while for paltry punk they roar and stickle,
They make it bawdier than a conventicle.

JOHN DRYDEN (1684)

'The Natives'
Prologue to Zobeide
spoken by Quick in the Character of a Sailor

In these bold times, when Learning's sons explore
The distant climate and the savage shore;
When wise Astronomers to India steer,
And quit for Venus, many a brighter here;
While Botanists, all cold to smiles and dimpling,
Forsake the fair, and patiently – go simpling;
When every bosom swells with wond'rous scenes,
Priests, cannibals, and hoity-toity queens:
Our bard into the general spirit enters,
And fits his little frigate for adventures:
With Scythian stores, and trinkets deeply laden,
He this way steers his course, in hopes of trading –
Yet ere he lands he 'as ordered me before,
To make an observation on the shore.
Where are we driven? our reck'ning sure is lost!
This seems a barren and a dangerous coast.
Lord, what a sultry climate am I under!
Yon ill foreboding cloud seems big with thunder.

(*Upper Gallery.*)

48

There Mangroves spread, and larger than I've seen 'em –

(*Pit.*)

Here trees of stately size – and turtles in 'em –

(*Balconies.*)

Here ill–condition'd oranges abound –

(*Stage.*)

And Apples, (*Takes up one and tastes it.*) bitter apples strew
   the ground.
The place is uninhabited, I fear!
I heard a hissing – there are serpents here!
O there the natives are – a dreadful race!
The men have tails, the women paint their face!
No doubt they're all barbarians. – Yes, 'tis so;
I'll try to make palaver with them though;

(*Making signs.*)

'Tis best, however, keeping at a distance.
Good Savages, our Captain craves assistance;
Our ship's well stor'd; – in yonder creek we've laid her;
His honour is no mercenary trader;
This is his first adventure; lend him aid,
Or you may chance to spoil a thriving trade.
His goods, he hopes, are prime, and brought from far,
Equally fit for gallantry and war.
What! no reply to promises so ample?
I'd best step back – and order up a sample.

OLIVER GOLDSMITH (1771)

'Good Gentle Audience'

I' faith I like the audience that frequenteth there
With much applause. A man shall not be choked
With stench of garlic, nor be pasted
To the barmy jacket of a beer-brewer.
. . . Tis a good gentle audience.

JOHN MARSTON (1600)

'Tis ten to one this play can never please
All that are here. Some come to take their ease
And sleep an act or two; but those, we fear,
W' have frighted with our trumpets . . .

WILLIAM SHAKESPEARE (1613)

. . . Somebody
Once pickt a pocket in this playhouse yard,
Was hoisted on the stage, and sham'd about it.

Nobody and Somebody (1593)

'Chatter Boxes'

Epilogue for *The Toy*, written for Miss Fontenelle

I han't much time to chatter here to you,
Yet take a hint of what I mean to do:
As Sol from clouds more brightly darts his rays,
So, long pent up, I'll burst into a blaze.
For dress, ton, life, I've a prodigious passion,
I'll make a pretty little woman of fashion.
Round the gay circle fly my cards about,
Sunday I fix on for th' enchanting rout.
At charming loo my company I set,
Or every heart beats high at dear piquette.
To nodding friends I'll in my chariot bob,
Splash up the dirt, and rattle through the mob.
Or in state chair my high head low I stoop,

My chin just popping out between my hoop: .
My six tall footmen strutting on before
Knock flambeaux round, and beat the *open* door.
Mind I'm a lady first, for, ere I marry,
My Hal shall promise that he'll be Sir Harry.
My pleasures quite in style, all brilliant, gay,
Yet still so vulgar as to like a play.
The playhouse crowded, how we're squeez'd and tumbled,
Box, pit, and gallery, such jargon jumbled!
So pleasant too the conversation round ye.
    (*Mimics the several characters.*)
'Are you there, Jack?'[1] 'Hah, Tom!'[2] 'The deuce confound ye!'[3]
'A charming girl, that yonder!'[4] 'La, what brutes!'[5]
'Is this seat taken?'[6] 'Dem your dirty boots!'[7]
'Were you at Ascot, ma'am?'[8] 'I go to races!'[9]
'Hey, shut the door, there!'[10] 'Lady Dumplin's places!'[11]
'Silence!'[12] Book o' the songs, ma'am?'[13] 'Ah, such
    nonsense!'[14]
'Hiss again, I'll knock you down!'[15] 'You!'[16] ''Pon my
    conscience.'[17]
'Wins Desdemona, Stories all he told her.'[18]
'Suddenly taken ill.'[19] 'Who's bottle-holder?'[20]
'Hip!'[21](*Sings.*) 'And you to bless this charming creature.'[22]
'Cursed hot.'[23] 'How cold!'[24] Open the ventilator.'[25]
'His Lordship went this morning, Sir, for Dover.'[26]
'A fine good-natured fellow!'[27] 'Throw him over!'[28]
'Take off your bonnet, Ma'am.'[29] 'He'll then adore me.'[30]
'I shan't sit down, 'till they sit down afore me.'[31]
'What act is this?'[32] 'I drank tea in Pall Mall.'[33]
'A brazen romp, that little Fontenelle!'[34] (*Bell rings.*)
My clack's cut short, for there's the prompter's bell.
    Good night, kind friends, to you, and you, and you!
    Here I could prate for ever – but Adieu!

JOHN O'KEEFFE (1826)

1 A sailor. 2 Another sailor. 3 Women in gallery. 4 Buck in the boxes. 5 Lady in green boxes. 6 Country gentleman. 7 Foppish officer. 8 Man of the turf. 9 Old lady. 10 Finical Fop. 11 Box-keeper. 12 Noisy fellow in upper gallery. 13 Fruit woman. 14 Critic. 15 Irishman. 16 Critic. 17 Irishman. 18 Citizen's wife in the pit. 19 Apologising Performer. 20 Pupil of Humphries. 21 Sailor. 22 Carlos, in Duenna. 23 Fat Citizen in pit. 24 Affected lady. 25 Man in gallery. 26 Man of Fashion in lower boxes. 27 Drunken Buck in upper boxes. 28 Men in slips. 29 Man in pit. 30 Frail Fair in upper boxes. 31 Yorkshireman. 32 Drunken man. 33 Fop. 34 A starched prude.

'Pat Jennings' Hat'

From 'The Theatre' in *Rejected Addresses*

Pat Jennings in the upper gallery sat,
But, leaning forward, Jennings lost his hat:
Down from the gallery the beaver flew,
And spurn'd the one to settle in the two.
How shall he act? Pay at the gallery door
Two shillings for what cost, when new, but four?
Or, till half-price, to save his shilling, wait,
And gain his hat again at half-past eight?
Now, while his fears anticipate a thief,
John Mullins whispers, 'Take my handkerchief.'
'Thank you,' cries Pat, 'but one won't make a line.'
'Take mine,' cried Wilson, and cried Stokes, 'take mine.'
A motley cable soon Pat Jennings ties,
Where Spitalfields with real India vies.
Like Iris' bow, down darts the painted hue,
Starr'd, striped, and spotted, yellow, red, and blue,
Old calico, torn silk, and muslin new.
George Green below, with palpitating hand,
Loops the last 'kerchief to the beaver's band –
Up soars the prize; the youth, with joy unfeign'd,
Regain'd the felt, and felt what he regain'd,
While to the applauding galleries grateful Pat
Made a low bow, and touch'd the ransom'd hat.

JAMES SMITH (1812)

To Miss Nelson on her Visit to Wells

Welcome admired Horatia to our Wells –
Thou pride of Burnham, and thou belle of belles!
Dull is that breast, that does not sigh for thee –
To love thee is but sensibility!

Oh for the poet's pen, the Muse's fire,
To say how much, how deeply I admire
Thy looks enchanting and thy graceful mien
By none with justice told, or safely seen –
In Wells, or Burnham, or where'er you rove,
The Graces follow with the God of Love –
With you in vain for fame a Fisher tries,
You conqu'ring win all hearts and charm all eyes –
You steal attention from the actor's skill,
The play forgot, you captivate the will –
In you transcendently becoming shine
The genuine virtues of the Nelson line!
Spirit with ease and gaiety combined –
The feeling heart with the unconquered mind,
Great Nelson prostrate laid a world of foes –
Thy charms have prostrate laid a world of beaux!

HENRI (1820)

The Boy in the Gallery

A Song

I'm a young girl and have just come over,
    Over from the country where they do things big;
And amongst the boys I've got a lover,
    And since I've got a lover, why I don't care a fig!

The boy I love is up in the gallery,
    The boy I love is looking now at me;
There he is can't you see? Waving his handkerchief,
    As merry as a robin that sings on the tree.

The boy that I love they call him a cobbler,
    But he's not a cobbler, allow me to state;
For Johnny is a tradesman, and he works in the Boro',
    Where they sole and heel them whilst you wait.

The boy I love, &c.

53

Now if I were a Duchess and had a lot of money,
   I'd give it to the boy that's going to marry me;
But I haven't got a penny so we'll live on love and kisses,
   And be just as happy as the birds on the tree.

The boy I love, &c.

GEORGE WARE (1885)

Chocolates

Here the seats are; George, old man,
Get some chocolates while you can.

Quick, the curtain's going to rise,
(Either Bradbury's or Spry's).

'*The Castle ramparts, Elsinore*'
(That's not sufficient, get some more).

There's the *Ghost*; he does look wan
(Help yourself, and pass them on).

Doesn't *Hamlet* do it well?
(This one is a caramel).

Polonius's beard is fine
(Don't you grab; that big one's mine).

Look the *King* can't bear the play
(Throw that squashy one away).

Now the *King* is at his prayers
(Splendid, there are two more layers).

Hamlet's going for his mother
(Come on, Tony, have another).

54

Poor *Ophelia*! Look, she's mad
(However many's Betty had?)

The *Queen* is dead and so's the *King*
(Keep that lovely silver string).

Now even *Hamlet* can no more
(Pig! You've dropped it on the floor).

That last Act's simply full of shocks
(There's several left, so bring the box).

GUY BOAS (1925)

The Audience

He seemed to have so much to say
   Into his neighbour's ear
That those about him found the play
   Impossible to hear.

Perceiving that he must be cowed,
   A man in front looked grim,
And, turning round, said 'Hush' so loud
   That I said 'Hush' to him.

Although I thought I said the word
   As softly as could be,
A lady just behind me heard
   And she said 'Hush' to me.

She made a penetrating sound
   Which caused a general stir,
And half a dozen men turned round
   And they said 'Hush' to her.

The whole House then looked black as death;
    You should have seen them flush
With anger as they all took breath
    Together and said 'Hush.'

GUY BOAS (1925)

Theatre of Varieties

Circle on circle the hanging gardens descend,
Sloping from upper darkness, each flower face
Open, turned to the light and laughter and life
Of the sun-like stage. And all the space between,
Like the hot fringes of a summer sky,
Is quick with trumpets, beats with the pulse of drums,
Athwart whose sultry thunders rise and fall
To call the nameless spade a spade, 'Divine
Zenocrate!' There are dark mysteries
Whose name is beauty, strange revelations called
Love, and a gulph of pleasure and of awe
Where words fall vain and wingless in the dark;
The seen Ineffable, the felt but all-Unknown
and Undescribed, is God. 'Divine, divine!'
The god-intoxicated shout goes up.
'Divine Zenocrate!'
'Father,' the terrible infant's voice is shrill,
'Say, father, why does the lady wear no skirts?'
She wears no skirts; God's eyes have never been brighter.
The face flowers open in her emanation.
She is the suave and curving Kingdom of Heaven
Made visible, and in her sugared song
The ear finds paradise. Divine, divine!
Her belly is like a mound of wheat, her breasts
Are towers, her hair like a flock of goats.
    Her foot is feat with diamond toes
    And she – divine Zenocrate –
    And she on legs of ruby goes.

56

The face flowers tremble in the rushing wind
Of her loud singing. A poet in the pit
Jots down in tears the words of her Siren song.
　　So every spirit as it is most pure,
　　And hath in it the more of heavenly light,
　　So it the rarer body doth procure
　　To habit in, and is more fairly dight
　　With cheerful grace and amiable sight:
　　For of the soul the body form doth take;
　　And soul is form and doth the body make.
'Now, boys, together. All with me,' she cries
Through the long sweet suspense of dominant chords;
'For of the soul,' her voice is paradise,
'For of the soul the body form doth take:
And soul is form and doth the body make.'
Zenocrate, alone, alone divine!

God save the King. Music's last practical joke
Still bugling in their ears of war and glory,
The folk emerge into the night.
Already next week's bills are being posted: —
Urim and Thummim, cross-talk comedians;
Of rose and rabbit, raiser from the dead —
To invade the sanctity of private life.

The Six Aerial Sisters Polpetini
Dive dangerously from trapeze to far
Trapeze, like stars, and know not how to fall.
For if they did and if, of his silver balls,
Sclopis, the juggler, dropped but one — but one
Of all the flying atoms which he builds
With his quick throwing into a solid arch —
What panic then would shake the pale flower faces
Blooming so tranquilly in their hanging beds!
What a cold blast of fear! But patrons must not,
And since they must not, cannot be alarmed.
Hence Sclopis, hence (the proof is manifest)
The Six Aerial Ones infallibly
Function, and have done, and for ever will.

Professor Chubb's Automaton performs
Upon the viols and virginals, plays chess,
Ombre and loo, mistigri, tric-trac, pushpin,
Sings Lilliburlero in falsetto, answers
All questions put to it, and with its rubber feet
Noiselessly dances the antique heydiguy.

'Is it a man?' the terrible infant wonders.
And 'no' they say, whose business it is
To say such infants nay. And 'no' again
They shout when, after watching Dobbs and Debs
Step simultaneously through intricate dances,
Hammer the same tune with their rattling clogs
In faultless unison, the infant asks,
'And they, are they machines?'
Music, the revelation and marvellous lie,
Rebuilds in the minds of all a suave and curving
Kingdom of Heaven, where the saxophone
Affirms everlasting loves, the drums deny
Death, and where great Tenorio, when he sings,
Makes Picardy bloom only with perfumed roses,
And never a rotting corpse in all its earth.
Play, music, play! In God's bright limelight eyes
An angel walks and with one rolling glance
Blesses each hungry flower in the hanging gardens.
'Divine,' they cry, having no words by which
Flute fountains and the swallow flight of strings.
Music, the revelation and marvellous lie!
On the bright trestles tumblers, tamers of beasts,
Dancers and clowns affirm their fury of life.

> 'The World-Renowned Van Hogen Mogen in
> The Master Mystery of Modern Times.'

He talks, he talks; more powerfully than even
Music his quick words hammer on men's minds.
'Observe this hat, ladies and gentlemen;

Empty, observe, empty as the universe
Before the Head for which this Hat is made
Was or could think. Empty, observe, observe.'
The rabbit kicks; a bunch of paper flowers
Blooms in the limelight; paper tape unrolls,
Endless, a clue. 'Ladies and gentlemen . . . '
Sharp, sharp on malleable minds his words
Hammer. The little Indian boy
Enters the basket. Bright, an Ethiop's sword
Transfixes it and bleeding is withdrawn.
Death draws and petrifies the watching faces.
'Ladies and gentlemen': the great Van Hogen Mogen
Smiles and is kind. A puddle of dark blood
Slowly expands. 'The irremediable
Has been and is no more.'
Empty of all but blood, the basket gapes.
'Arise!' he calls, and blows his horn. 'Arise!'
And bird-like from the highest gallery
The little Indian answers.
Shout upon shout, the hanging gardens reverberate.
Happy because the irremediable is healed,
Happy because they have seen the impossible,
Because they are freed from the dull daily law,
They shout, they shout. And great Van Hogen Mogen
Modestly bows, graciously smiles. The band
Confirms the lie with cymbals and bassoons,
The curtain falls. How quickly the walls recede,
How soon the petrified gargoyles re-become
Women and men! who fill the warm thick air
With rumour of their loves and discontents,
Not suffering even great Hogen Mogen –
Only begetter out of empty hats
Ringpok, the Magian of Tibet;
The Two Bedelias; Ruby and Truby Dix;
Sam Foy and Troupe of Serio-Comic Cyclists . . .

Theatre of immemorial varieties,
Old mummery, but mummers never the same!
Twice nightly every night from now till doomsday
The hanging gardens, bedded with pale flower faces,
Young flowers in the old old gardens, will echo
With ever new, with ever new delight.

ALDOUS HUXLEY (1931)

To an Actress

I read your name when you were strange to me,
Where it stood blazoned bold with many more;
I passed it vacantly, and did not see
Any great glory in the shape it wore.

O cruelty, the insight barred me then!
Why did I not possess me with its sound,
And in its cadence catch and catch again
Your nature's essence floating thereabound?

Could *that* man be this I, unknowing you,
When now the knowing you is all of me,
And the old world of then is now a new,
And purpose no more what it used to be –
A thing of formal journeywork, but due
To springs that then were sealed up utterly?

THOMAS HARDY (1867)

To the Members of the Audience

You who look on while I work;
You who relax in the stalls;
What do you know of my life?
What do you know of it all?
You probably think I am rich;
From experience I know you suspect
My life is luxurious and wild –
I wish I could say: 'That's correct!'
Sometimes you boo what I do,
Sitting there in your comfort and ease,
But the worst that I do – this has been said before –
Is to fail when trying to please.
I am selfish at times I am sure,
(Though loved by my children and wife)
But, you who look on while I work,
What do you know of my life?

NICHOLAS SMITH (1962)

On Judging

You artists who, for pleasure or for pain
Deliver yourselves up to the judgement of the audience
Be moved in future
To deliver up also to the judgement of the audience
The world which you show.

You should show what is; but also
In showing what is you should suggest what could be and is
    not
And might be helpful. For from your portrayal
The audience must learn to deal with what is portrayed.
Let this learning be pleasurable. Learning must be taught
As an art, and you should
Teach dealing with things and with people
As an art too, and the practice of art is pleasurable.

To be sure, you live in a dark time. You see man
Tossed back and forth like a ball by evil forces.
Only an idiot lives without worry. The unsuspecting
Are already destined to go under. What were the
    earthquakes
Of grey prehistory compared to the afflictions
Which we suffer in cities? What were bad harvests
To the need that ravages us in the midst of plenty?

                    BERTOLT BRECHT (1938)
                    (Trans. Edith Anderson)

An Old Woman Outside the Abbey Theatre

In this theayter they has plays
    On us, and high–up people comes
And pays to see things playin' here
    They'd run like hell from in the slums.

            L A G STRONG (1923)

The Audience at the Court Theatre

They're the Pioneers of Progress, they're the Devotees of
    Art,
They're the men with bulging foreheads, they're a race of
    souls apart;
No ordinary drama can rely on their support –
It is Culture – yes, sir, Culture that they ask for at the
    Court.

Lesser men may like the plays that are produced for vulgar
    gain;
Lesser men may laugh at Huntley or be charmed by
    Edmund Payne;
But the audience would crush you with one vast, indignant
    snort,
If you showed such plays or mummers any evening at the
    Court.

But you must not think that every form of fun would come
    to grief;
They enjoy tuberculosis as a humorous relief.
And a really comic death–scene will infallibly extort
Tears of unaffected laughter from an audience at the Court.

Ah, but what they really revel in is something dark and
    grim.
If the hero kills his mother, or his mother murders him;
If loud shrieks ('off left') suggest that blood is flowing by
    the quart,
Then a placid satisfaction soothes the audience at the Court.

How they love it when a character brings out a gleaming
    knife,
Or kicks the prostrate body of his unoffending wife!
Such events come all too seldom, and such scenes are all too
    short
For the reckless, ruthless audience you meet with at the
    Court.

And when the play is ended, o'er a grateful cup of tea,
They discuss hot buns and Culture at the local ABC.
Then each journeys off to Balham or his Wimbledon resort,
Much refreshed in mind and spirit by his visit to the Court.

P G WODEHOUSE (1907)

A Midsummer Night's Dream
In Regent's Park

And what will they remember when
They wake, like Bottom, from their dream?
Will they believe they laughed like this?
And will their restless bodies seem
The same that settled here like dew
Along the benches, in a trance
Of hope and wonder, while old Puck
Led the four lovers through their dance?

The treetops rustle, and the sky
Darkens around a haughty moon.
Cartoon words on homespun lips
Float through the night in their balloon.
Titania curses Oberon
And up the loyal fairies leap.
Within a wood within a wood
The four enchanted lovers sleep.

And will these children ever think
Again about this leaf-lit scene –
Even a single turning branch
Glimmer in their darker green?
Perhaps one moment when the sky
Was dropping dusk light from above
Will touch their eyes with tenderness
Before another night of love.

DERWENT MAY (1977)

Curtain-Fall at the Ballet

The ballet sweeps to its finale
And the music governs everything.
As it surges over the isthmus between
The two kingdoms, the gods and goddesses extend
Their limbs, their hair, their impassioned gestures,
Till the sound-waves gather together in the dominant
Which crashes in finality on the green beach.

Then the red light glows and from overhead
I turn the windlass and divide
The worshippers from their glimpse of paradise,
With a wall of garnet velvet raised and lowered
While they shout hosannas and throw votive flowers.
The lights grow in the temple.

Down behind the curtain
I see the gods whisk off their golden hair
And disperse along corridors to their cells,
While before it, little girls run up and down the aisles
Buying plastic beakers of artificial squash.

The fiddlers start anew by playing A together
Till the gods return in new guises; the votaries converge;
And I see both sides from above, and observe how
People stay together by being parted from time to time.

JONATHAN FIELD (1971)

65

'Curtain Fall'

Epilogue to A Midsummer Night's Dream

If we shadows have offended,
Think but this, and all is mended,
That you have but slumb'red here
While these visions did appear.
And this weak and idle theme,
No more yielding but a dream,
Gentles, do not reprehend.
If you pardon, we will mend.
And, as I am an honest Puck,
If we have unearned luck
Now to scape the serpent's tongue,
We will make amends ere long;
Else the Puck a liar call.
So, good night unto you all.
Give me your hands, if we be friends,
And Robin shall restore amends.

WILLIAM SHAKESPEARE (*c* 1600)

The play is done; the curtain drops,
    Slow falling to the prompter's bell:
A moment yet the actor stops,
    And looks around to say farewell.
It is an irksome word and task:
    And when he's laughed and said his say,
He shows as he removes his mask,
    A face that's anything but gay.

W M THACKERAY (1848)

Children Leaving a Pantomime

Islands are places the sea would have eaten long ago
With it rolling and roaring for more like pantomime devils

Had not everything come right in the last scene
Before the walk-down and the wicked been sent empty
   away in repentant surprise.

The matinee watchers of Sinbads, Whittingtons, Crusoes
Are those small ones who know islands are lonely places,
Are for the existers and the enduring people.

These tumble downstairs to the exits of theatres
After a pantomime, know navigations are not only

To islands, but to selves, that the Lost Wood
Is not the outside-night-dark-haunted-owl-cried-trees

But is the inside-Lost-Wood-under-the-Sea surging nightly
And formidable around the small bed clothes.

Help those who walk slowly, polite and still half-lost in the
   show
Down long stairs from circle to foyer,

Held still inside the dream inside the dream.

See in the unseeing eye another who sees
The sea knock endlessly at the privacy of islands.

Hears movements of stones and the call of seabirds.
Help those who – blind with feeling and small –

Stumble with hand held helpfully out, back down to earth,
Who grow up later to know islands are hard personal places
   hardly won,

Where the sea strikes always at each regular tide
And harsh things happen, needing a magic to survive
  stronger than pantomime.

Help those who live now on the mainland where the earth is
  flat,
The pavement smooth and traffic breaks in like an obscene
  noise

Upon the silence in which people say goodbye to love,
Where lovers and would-be kind family ask bright
  impossible questions about the magic

Like, 'Did you enjoy it, darling? Was it nice?'

STEPHEN SURREY (1975)

At the Stage Door

Kicking my heels in the street,
Here at the edge of the pavement I wait for you, sweet,
Here in the crowd, the blent noises, blurred lights, of the
  street.

Under the archway sheer,
Sudden and black as a hole in the placarded wall,
Faces flicker and veer,
Wavering out of the darkness into the light,
Wavering back into night;
Under the archway, suddenly seen, the curls
And thin, bright faces of girls,
Roving eyes, and smiling lips, and the glance
Seeking, finding perchance,
Here at the edge of the pavement, there by the wall,
One face, out of them all.

Steadily, face after face,
Cheeks with the blush of the paint yet lingering, eyes
Still with their circle of black . . .
But hers, but hers?
Rose-leaf cheeks, and flower-soft lips, and the grace
Of the vanishing Spring come back,
And a child's heart blithe in the sudden and sweet surprise,
Slightly expectant, that shines
In the smile of her heart to my heart, of her eyes to my
    eyes.

ARTHUR SYMONS (1895)

X is for Exit. And now let us sing,
since he can't save the theatre, God save the King.

HUMBERT WOLFE (1932)

After a Play

The wind in spasms swept the street
As we walked very quietly
Till cold and silence seemed to meet
And make one point – one star set free
Between two stormy clouds. We leant
Upon both wind and words we meant.

A tense and joyful audience had
Thronged in the theatre we left.
Lovers had laughed at being sad
And justice, mercy were bereft
Of all abstractions. So were we,
Talking so low yet passionately.

ELIZABETH JENNINGS (1975)

PLAYWRIGHTS

He was reviled, he was revered –
But he was Shelley in a beard!

ANON (1928)

Ahenobarbus
at Rehearsal.

To Make a Play

To make a play
is to make people,
to make people do
what you say;

to make real people
do and say
what you make;
to make people make

what you say real;
to make real
people make up
and do what you

make up. What you
make makes people
come and see
what people do

and say, and then
go away and do
what they see –
and see what

they do. Real
people do and say,
and you see and
make up people;

people come to see
what you do.
They see what *they*
do, and they

may go away undone.
You can make
people, or you
can unmake. You

can do or you
can undo. People
you make up make up
and make people;

people come to
see – to see
themselves real,
and they go away

and do what you
say – as if they
were made up,
and wore makeup.

To make a play
is to make
people; to make
people make

themselves; to
make people
make themselves
new. So real.

The Craftsman

Once, after long-drawn revel at The Mermaid,
He to the overbearing Boanerges
Jonson, uttered (if half of it were liquor,
                    Blessed be the vintage!)

Saying how, at an alehouse under Cotswold,
He had made sure of his very Cleopatra,
Drunk with enormous, salvation-contemning
                    Love for a tinker.

How, while he hid from Sir Thomas's keepers,
Crouched in a ditch and drenched by the midnight
Dews, he had listened to gipsy Juliet
                    Rail at the dawning.

How at Bankside, a boy drowning kittens
Winced at the business; whereupon his sister –
Lady Macbeth aged seven – thrust 'em under,
                    Sombrely scornful.

How on a Sabbath, hushed and compassionate –
She being known since her birth to the townsfolk –
Stratford dredged and delivered from Avon
                    Dripping Ophelia.

So, with a thin third finger marrying
Drop to wine-drop domed on the table,
Shakespeare opened his heart till the sunrise
                    Entered to hear him.

London waked and he, imperturbable,
Passed from waking to hurry after shadows . . .
Busied upon shows of no earthly importance?
                    Yes, but he knew it!

RUDYARD KIPLING (1919)

Christopher Marlowe

From *An Elegy to Henry Reynolds:*
Of Poets and Poesy

Next Marlowe, bathed in the Thespian springs,
Had in him those brave translunary things
That your first poets had; his raptures were
All air and fire, which made his verses clear;
For that fine madness still he did retain,
Which rightly should possess a poet's brain.

MICHAEL DRAYTON (1627)

The time has been when plays were not so plenty,
And a less number now would well content ye.
New plays did then like almanacks appear,
And one was thought sufficient for a year.

WILLIAM CONGREVE (1697)

Lines on the Mermaid Tavern

From a letter to Ben Jonson

Methinks the little wit I had is lost
Since I saw you, for wit is like a rest
Held up at tennis, which men do the best,
With the best gamesters. What things have we seen,
Done at the Mermaid! Heard words that have been
So nimble, and so full of subtle flame
As if that every one from whence they came,
Had meant to put his whole wit in a jest,
And had resolved to live a fool, the rest
Of his dull life; then when there hath been thrown
Wit able enough to justify the town
For three days past, wit that might warrant be
For the whole city to talk foolishly

Till that were cancelled, and when that was gone,
We left an air behind us, which alone,
Was able to make the two next companies
Right witty; though but downright fools, more wise.

FRANCIS BEAUMONT (c 1610)

'Further Lines on the Mermaid Tavern'

Souls of Poets dead and gone,
What Elysium have ye known,
Happy field or mossy cavern,
Choicer than the Mermaid Tavern?
Have ye tippled drink more fine
Than mine host's Canary wine?
Or are fruits of Paradise
Sweeter than those dainty pies
Of venison? O generous food!
Drest as though bold Robin Hood
Would, with his maid Marian,
Sup and bowse from horn and can.

I have heard that on a day
Mine host's sign-board flew away,
Nobody knew whither, till
An astrologer's old quill
To a sheepskin gave the story,
Said he saw you in your glory,
Underneath a new old sign
Sipping beverage divine,
And pledging with contented smack
The Mermaid in the Zodiac.

Souls of Poets dead and gone,
What Elysium have ye known,
Happy field or mossy cavern,
Choicer than the Mermaid Tavern?

JOHN KEATS (1820)

Upon Master Fletcher's Dramatical Works

What? Now the stage is down dar'st thou appear
Bold Fletcher in this tott'ring hemisphere?
Yes; poets are like palms which, the more weight
You cast upon them, grow more strong and straight;
'Tis not love's thunderbolt, nor Mars his spear,
Or Neptune's angry trident, poets fear.

Had now grim Ben been breathing, with what rage,
And high-swoln fury had he lash'd this age;
Shakespeare with Chapman had gone mad, and torn
Their gentle sock, and lofty buskins worn,
To make their Muse welter up to the chin
In blood; of fained scenes no need have been,
England like Lucian's eagle with an arrow
Of her own plumes piercing her heart quite thorough,
Had been a theatre and subject fit
To exercise in real truths their wit.

Yet none like high-winged Fletcher had been found
This eagle's tragic destiny to sound,
Rare Fletcher's quill had soar'd up to the sky,
And drawn down gods to see the tragedy.
Live famous dramatist, let every spring
Make thy bay flourish, and fresh burgeons bring:
And since we cannot have thee trod o' th' stage,
We will applaud thee in this silent page.

I A HOWELL (1647)

Five years after the closing of the public playhouses by order of Parliament in 1642, an enterprising printer published in full the *Comedies and Tragedies* of the ever popular Francis Beaumont (c 1584–1616) and John Fletcher (1597–1625). This poem is one of the many commendatory pieces that prefaced the volume.

Ode

Written on the blank page before
Beaumont and Fletcher's tragi-comedy,
The Fair Maid of the Inn

Bards of Passion and of Mirth,
Ye have left your souls on earth!
Have ye souls in heaven too,
Double lived in regions new?
Yes, and those of heaven commune
With the spheres of sun and moon;
With the noise of fountains wond'rous,
And the parle of voices thund'rous;
With the whisper of heaven's trees
And one another, in soft ease
Seated on Elysian lawns
Brows'd by none but Dian's fawns;
Underneath large blue-bells tented,
Where the daisies are rose-scented,
And the rose herself has got
Perfume which on earth is not;
Where the nightingale doth sing
Not a senseless, tranced thing,
But divine melodious truth;
Philosophic numbers smooth;
Tales and golden histories
Of heaven and its mysteries.

Thus ye live on high, and then
On the earth ye live again;
And the souls ye left behind you
Teach us, here, the way to find you,
Where your other souls are joying,
Never slumber'd, never cloying.
Here, your earth-born souls still speak
To mortals, of their little week;

Of their sorrows and delights;
Of their passions and their spites;
Of their glory and their shame;
What doth strengthen and what maim.
Thus ye teach us, every day
Wisdom, though fled far away.

Bards of Passion and of Mirth,
Ye have left your souls on earth!
Ye have souls in heaven too,
Double-lived in regions new!

JOHN KEATS (1820)

To the Memory of My Beloved Master William Shakespeare, and What He Hath Left Us

To draw no envy, Shakespeare, on thy name,
Am I thus ample to thy book and fame;
While I confess thy writings to be such,
As neither Man nor Muse can praise too much.
'Tis true, and all men's suffrage. But these ways
Were not the paths I meant unto thy praise;
For seeliest ignorance on these may light,
Which, when it sounds at best, but echoes right;
Or blind affection, which doth ne'er advance
The truth, but gropes, and urgeth all by chance;
Or crafty malice might pretend this praise,
And think to ruin where it seemed to raise.
These are, as some infamous bawd or whore
Should praise a matron; what could hurt her more?
But thou are proof against them, and, indeed,
Above the ill fortune of them, or the need.

I therefore will begin: Soul of the age!
The applause! delight! the wonder of our stage!

My Shakespeare rise! I will not lodge thee by
Chaucer, or Spenser, or bid Beaumont lie
A little further, to make thee a room:
Thou art a monument, without a tomb,
And art alive still while thy book doth live
And we have wits to read, and praise to give.
That I not mix thee so my brain excuses,
I mean with great, but disproportioned Muses:
For if I thought my judgement were of years,
I should commit thee surely with thy peers,
And tell how far thou didst our Lyly outshine,
Or sporting Kyd, or Marlowe's mighty line.

And though thou hadst small Latin and less Greek,
From thence to honour thee, I would not seek
For names: but call forth thund'ring Aeschylus,
Euripides, and Sophocles to us,
Pacuvius, Accius, him of Cordova dead,
To life again, to hear thy buskin tread
And shake a stage; or when thy socks were on,
Leave thee alone for the comparison
Of all that insolent Greece or haughty Rome
Sent forth, or since did from their ashes come.
Triumph, my Britain, thou hast one to show,
To whom all Scenes of Europe homage owe.
He was not of an age, but for all time!
And all the Muses still were in their prime,
When, like Apollo, he came forth to warm
Our ears, or like a Mercury to charm!
Nature herself was proud of his designs,
And joyed to wear the dressing of his lines!
Which were so richly spun, and woven so fit,
As since, she will vouchsafe no other wit.
The merry Greek, tart Aristophanes,
Neat Terence, witty Plautus, now not please;
But antiquated and deserted lie,
As they were not of Nature's family.

Yet must I not give Nature all; thy Art,
My gentle Shakespeare, must enjoy a part.
For though the poet's matter nature be,
His art doth give the fashion: and, that he
Who casts to write a living line, must sweat,
(Such as thine are) and strike the second heat
Upon the Muses' anvil; turn the same,
And himself with it, that he thinks to frame;
Or for the laurel he may gain a scorn;
For a good poet's made as well as born.
And such wert thou! Look how the father's face
Lives in his issue, even so the race
Of Shakespeare's mind and manners brightly shines
In his well turned and true filed lines:
In each of which he seems to shake a lance,
As brandisht at the eyes of ignorance.

Sweet Swan of Avon! what a sight it were
To see thee in our waters yet appear,
And make those flights upon the banks of Thames,
That so did take Eliza and our James!
But stay, I see thee in the hemisphere
Advanced, and made a constellation there!
Shine forth, thou Star of Poets, and with rage,
Or influence, chide or cheer the drooping stage,
Which, since thy flight from hence, hath mourned like
    night,
And despairs day but for thy volume's light.

                              BEN JONSON (1623)

    Then to the well-trod stage anon,
    If Jonson's learned sock be on,
    Or sweetest Shakespeare, Fancy's child,
    Warble his native wood-notes wild.

                    JOHN MILTON (1632)

81

On the Site of a Mulberry-Tree
planted by Wm Shakespeare, felled by the Rev F Gastrell

This tree, here fall'n, no common birth or death
Shared with its kind. The world's enfranchised son,
Who found the trees of Life and Knowledge one,
Here set it, frailer than his laurel-wreath.
Shall not the wretch whose hand it fell beneath
Rank also singly – the supreme unhung?
Lo! Sheppard, Turpin, pleading with black tongue
This viler thief's unsuffocated breath!
We'll search thy glossary, Shakespeare! whence almost,
And whence alone, some name shall be reveal'd
For this deaf drudge, to whom no length of ears
Sufficed to catch the music of the spheres;
Whose soul is carrion now – too mean to yield
Some Starveling's ninth allotment of a ghost.

DANTE GABRIEL ROSSETTI (1853)

On Shakespeare

What needs my Shakespeare for his honoured bones
The labour of an age in piled stones?
Or that his hallowed reliques should be hid
Under a star-ypointing pyramid?
Dear son of memory, great heir of fame,
What need'st thou such weak witness of thy name?
Thou in our wonder and astonishment
Hast built thyself a livelong monument.
For whilst, to the shame of slow-endeavouring art,
Thy easy numbers flow, and that each heart

Hath from the leaves of thy unvalued book
Those Delphic lines with deep impression took,
Then thou, our fancy of itself bereaving,
Dost make us marble with too much conceiving,
And so sepulchred in such pomp dost lie
That kings for such a tomb would wish to die.

JOHN MILTON (1630)

The Shakespeare Memorial

Lord Lilac thought it rather rotten
That Shakespeare should be quite forgotten,
And therefore got on a Committee
With several chaps out of the City,
And Shorter and Sir Herbert Tree,
Lord Rothschild and Lord Rosebery,
And F C G and Comyns Carr,
Two dukes and a dramatic star,
Also a clergyman now dead;
And while the vain world careless sped
Unheeding the heroic name –
The souls most fed with Shakespeare's flame
Still sat unconquered in a ring,
Remembering him like anything.

G K CHESTERTON (c 1915)

archy confesses

coarse
jocosity
catches the crowd
shakespeare
and i
are often
low browed

the fish wife
curse
and the laugh
of the horse
shakespeare
and i
are frequently
coarse

aesthetic
excuses
in bill s behalf
are adduced
to refine
big bill s
coarse laugh

but bill
he would chuckle
to hear such guff
he pulled
rough stuff
and he liked
rough stuff

hoping you
are the same

archy

DON MARQUIS (1927)

Sonnet for Shakespeare

Was it the Muse or the soft voice of Avon
That acted quickener, the heart or head,
Tongue, hand or brain – or what else under Heaven
That bid the plays be made, the words be said?
What's poetry? What stirs and what is stirred?
Where do the winds of inspiration rise
And what awakened sense, ascending bird,
Is moved to move, and climbs the air, and flies?

Now is the word made world, the senses, flame,
And all of time seen in the poet's glance:
What all's becoming and what all became.
Now this, a self-perpetuating dance,
Finds meaning. So he celebrates our span
On earth and ever lights the path of man.

BRYAN STOCKS (1964)

An Elegy on Ben Jonson

WHO first reform'd our stage with justest laws,
And was the first best judge in his own cause,
Who, when his actors trembled for applause,

Could, with a noble confidence, prefer
His own, by right, to a noble theatre;
From principles, which he knew could not err.

Who to his fable did his persons fit,
With all the properties of art and wit,
And above all that could be acted, writ.

Who public follies did to covert drive,
Which he again could cunningly retrieve,
Leaving them no ground to rest on, and thrive.

Here JONSON lies, whom had I nam'd before,
In that one word alone I had paid more,
Than can be now, when plenty makes me poor.

JOHN CLEVELAND (1638)

Ode to Himself

Come leave the loathed stage,
And the more loathsome age,
Where pride and impudence in faction knit,
Usurp the chair of wit:
Inditing and arraigning every day,
Something they call a play.
Let their fastidious vain
Commission of the brain
Run on, and rage, sweat, censure, and condemn,
They were not made for thee, less thou for them.

Say that thou pour'st 'em wheat,
And they would acorns eat:
'Twere simple fury, still thyself to waste
On such as have no taste:
To offer them a surfeit of pure bread,
Whose appetites are dead:
No, give them grains their fill,
Husks, draff to drink, and swill:
If they love lees, and leave the lusty wine,
Envy them not, their palate's with the swine.

No doubt a mouldy tale,
Like *Pericles*, and stale
As the shrive's crusts, and nasty as his fish,
Scraps out of every dish,
Thrown forth and rak'd into the common tub,
May keep up the play club.
Broom's sweepings do as well
There, as his master's meal:
For who the relish of these guests will fit,
Needs set them but the alms-basket of wit.

And much good do 't ye then,
    Brave plush and velvet men
Can feed on orts; and safe in your scene clothes,
    Dare quit upon your oaths
The stagers, and the stage-writes too, your peers,
    Of stuffing your large ears
    With rage of comic socks,
    Wrought upon twenty blocks;
Which if they're torn and foul, and patch'd enough.
    The gamesters share your guilt, and you their stuff.

    Leave things so prostitute,
    And take th' Alcaic lute;
Or thine own Horace, or Anacreon's lyre;
    Warm thee by Pindar's fire:
And though thy nerves be shrunk, and blood be cold,
    Ere years have made thee old,
    Strike that disdainful heat
    Throughout, to their defeat:
As curious fools, and envious of thy strain,
May blushing swear, no palsy's in thy brain.

    But when they hear thee sing,
    The glories of the King;
His zeal to God, and his just awe o'er men,
    They may, blood-shaken, then
Feel such a flesh-quake to possess their powers,
    That no tun'd harp like ours,
    In sound of peace or wars,
    Shall truly hit the stars:
When they shall read the acts of Charles his reign,
And see his chariot triumph 'bove his Wain.

BEN JONSON (1631)

87

'The Infection'

From the Epilogue to *The Pilgrim*

Perhaps the Parson stretch'd a point too far,
When with our *Theatres* he wag'd a war.
He tells you, that this very moral age
Receiv'd the first infection from the stage.
But sure, a banisht Court, with lewdness fraught,
The seeds of open vice returning brought.
Thus lodg'd, (as vice by great example thrives)
It first debauch'd the daughters and the wives.
London, a fruitful soil, yet never bore
So plentiful a crop of horns before.
The *Poets*, who must live by Courts or starve,
Were proud, so good a government to serve;
And mixing with buffons and pimps profane,
Tainted the stage, for some small snip of gain.

JOHN DRYDEN (1700)

Keen satire is the business of the stage.

GEORGE FARQUHAR (1707)

'Name Dropping'

Our modern poets to that pass are driven,
Those names are curtail'd which they first had given;
And, as we wisht to have their memories drown'd,
We scarcely can afford them half their sound.

Greene, who had in both Academies ta'en
Degree of Master, yet could never gain
To be call'd more than Robin: who, had he
Profest aught save the Muse, serv'd and been free
After a seven years prenticeship, might have
(With credit too) gone Robert to his grave.

Marlowe, renown'd for his rare art and wit,
Could ne'er attain beyond the name of Kit,
Although his *Hero and Leander* did
Merit addition rather. Famous Kyd
Was call'd but Tom. Tom Watson, though he wrote
Able to make Apollo's self to dote
Upon his Muse, for all that he could strive,
Yet never could to his full name arrive.

Tom Nash (in his time of no small esteem)
Could not a second syllable redeem.
Excellent Beaumont, in the foremost rank
Of the rar'st wits, was never more than Frank.
Mellifluous Shakespeare, whose enchanting quill
Commanded mirth or passion, was but Will.

And famous Jonson, though his learned pen
Be dipt in Castaly, is still but Ben.
Fletcher and Webster, of that learned pack
None of the mean'st, yet neither was but Jack.
Dekker's but Tom; nor May, nor Middleton.
And he's but now Jack Ford, that once was John.

THOMAS HEYWOOD (1635)

'A Play is Wrought'

First Prologue to *Secret Love, or The Maiden Queen*

He who writ this, not without pains and thought
From French and English theatres has brought
Th' exactest rules by which a play is wrought.

The Unities of Action, Place, and Time;
The scenes unbroken; and a mingled chime
Of Jonson's humour, with Corneille's rhyme.

But while dead colours he with care did lay,
He fears his wit, or plot, he did not weigh,
Which are the living beauties of a play.

Plays are like towns, which howe'er fortifi'd
By engineers, have still some weaker side
By the o'erseen defendant unespied.

And with that art you make approaches now;
Such skilful fury in assaults you show,
That every poet without shame may bow.

Ours therefore humbly would attend your doom,
If soldier-like, he may have terms to come
With flying colours and with beat of drum.

JOHN DRYDEN (1667)

Yet to write plays is easy, faith, enough,
As you have seen by Cibber in *Tartuffe*.
With how much wit he did your heads engage!
He only stole the play – he writ the title-page.

GEORGE SEWELL (1719)

'The Drama's Laws'

Spoken by David Garrick at the reopening of the
Theatre Royal, Drury Lane, 1747

When Learning's triumph o'er her barb'rous foes
First rear'd the stage, immortal Shakespeare rose;
Each change of many-colour'd life he drew,
Exhausted worlds, and then imagin'd new:
Existence saw him spurn her bounded reign,
And panting Time toil'd after him in vain.
His pow'rful strokes presiding Truth impress'd,
And unresisted Passion storm'd the breast.
Then Jonson came, instructed from the school,
To please in method, and invent by rule;
His studious patience and laborious art,
By regular approach assail'd the heart:
Cold Approbation gave the ling'ring bays,
For those, who durst not censure, scarce could praise.
A mortal born, he met the gen'ral doom,
But left, like Egypt's kings, a lasting tomb.

The wits of Charles found easier way to fame,
Nor wish'd for Jonson's art, or Shakespeare's flame.
Themselves they studied, as they felt they writ;
Intrigue was plot, obscenity was wit.
Vice always found a sympathetic friend;
They pleas'd their age, and did not aim to mend.
Yet bards like these aspir'd to lasting praise,
And proudly hoped to pimp in future days.
Their case was gen'ral, their supports were strong,
Their slaves were willing, and their reign was long:
Till Shame regain'd the post that Sense betray'd,
And Virtue call'd Oblivion to her aid.

Then crush'd by rules, and weaken'd as refined,
For years the power of Tragedy declined;
From bard to bard the frigid caution crept,
Till Declamation roar'd whilst Passion slept;
Yet still did Virtue deign the stage to tread,
Philosophy remain'd, though Nature fled.
But forc'd, at length, her ancient reign to quit,
She saw great Faustus lay the ghost of Wit;
Exulting Folly hailed the joyful day,
And Pantomime and Song confirm'd her sway.

But who the coming changes can presage,
And mark the future periods of the Stage?
Perhaps, if skill could distant times explore,
New Behns, new Durfeys, yet remain in store;
Perhaps where Lear has rav'd, and Hamlet died,
On flying cars new sorcerers may ride:
Perhaps (for who can guess th' effects of chance?)
Here Hunt may box or Mahomet may dance.
Hard is his lot that here by Fortune plac'd,
Must watch the wild vicissitudes of taste;
With ev'ry meteor of caprice must play,
And chase the new-blown bubbles of the day.

Ah! let not Censure term our fate our choice,
The stage but echoes back the public voice;
The drama's laws, the drama's patrons give,
For we that live to please, must please to live.
Then prompt no more the follies you decry,
As tyrants doom their tools of guilt to die;
'Tis yours, this night, to bid the reign commence
Of rescued Nature and reviving Sense;
To chase the charms of sound, the pomp of show
For useful Mirth and salutary Woe;
Bid scenic Virtue form the rising age,
And Truth diffuse her radiance from the stage.

SAMUEL JOHNSON (1747)

'The Singing Ghost'

From *A Hamlet Travestie in Three Acts*
to the tune of *Giles Scroggins' Ghost*

GHOST (*sings*):

Behold in me your father's sprite. Ri tol tiddy lol de ray,
Doom'd for a term to walk the night. Tiddy, tiddy, &c.
You'll scarce believe me when I say,
That I'm bound to fast in fires all day,
Till my crimes are burnt and purg'd away. Ri tol tiddy, &c.

But that I am forbid to blow. Ri tol tiddy, &c.
The dreadful secrets which I know. Tiddy, tiddy, &c.
I could such a dismal tale unfold,
As would make your precious blood run cold!
But ah! those things must not be told. Ri tol tiddy, &c.

Your father suddenly you miss'd. Ri tol tiddy, &c.
I'll tell you how: List! List! O list! Tiddy, tiddy &c.
'Twas given out to all the town,
That a serpent pull'd your father down –
But now that serpent wears his crown. Ri tol tiddy, &c.

Your uncle is the man I mean. Ri tol tiddy, &c.
That diddled me out of my crown and my queen. Tiddy,
    tiddy, &c.
O what a falling off was there!
But brief let me be, I must back repair,
For methinks I scent the morning air. Ri tol tiddy, &c.

One afternoon as was my use. Ri tol tiddy, &c.
I went to my orchard to take a snooze. Tiddy, tiddy, &c.
When your uncle into my ear did pour
A bottle of cursed hellebore.
How little did I think I should wake no more! Ri tol tiddy, &c.

Doom'd by a brother's hand was I. Ri tol tiddy, &c.
To lose my crown, my wife, to die. Tiddy, tiddy, &c.
I should like to have settled my worldly affairs,
But the rascal came on so unawares,
That I hadn't even time to say my prayers. Ri tol tiddy, &c.

Torment your uncle for my sake. Ri tol tiddy, &c.
Let him never be at peace, asleep or awake. Tiddy, tiddy, &c.
Your mother's plague let her conscience be –
But I must be off for the daylight I see.
Adieu, adieu, adieu! Remember me! Ri tol tiddy, &c.

(*The* GHOST *descends.*)

HAMLET:

Remember thee! – I feel in such a flurry,
Egad, I shan't forget thee in a hurry.
Remember thee! Yes, from my souvenir,
All memoranda swift shall disappear;
There thy commandment all alone I'll write;
And if e'er I forget thee – blow me tight.

JOHN POOLE (1810)

'Garrick Assesses Shakespeare'

His plays are out of joint – O cursed spite!
That ever I was born to set them right!

ARTHUR MURPHY (1772)

When I Read Shakespeare —

When I read Shakespeare I am struck with wonder
that such trivial people should muse and thunder
in such lovely language.

Lear, the old buffer, you wonder his daughters
didn't treat him rougher,
the old chough, the old chuffer!

And Hamlet, how boring, how boring to live with,
so mean and self-conscious, blowing and snoring
his wonderful speeches, full of other folks' whoring!

And Macbeth and his Lady, who should have been choring,
such suburban ambition, so messily goring
old Duncan with daggers!

How boring, how small Shakespeare's people are!
Yet the language so lovely! like the dyes from gas-tar.

D H LAWRENCE (1929)

All's Well That Ends
or, Shakespeare Unmasked

I'm afraid he'll have to go.
He won't pass muster these days.

Black men he didn't like: he made them
Proud and gullible and jealous and black
(Good fighters, but otherwise out of their depth).
He didn't like women, but neither
Was he a frank and manly homosexual.

'Woman delights not me: no, nor man neither . . .'
As for Jews, his complaint was that they were
Interested in money, were not Christians, and
If you pricked them they bled all over the place.
They deserved to have their daughters make
Unsuitable marriages.

(Put like that, Jews sound like a lot of us.
I shall have to rewrite this bit.)

A very dangerous man.
Think of all the trouble caused by that
Thoroughly offensive play of his, *Coriolanus*.
One night it wounded the feelings of the fascists,
The next it wounded the feelings of the communists.

He was anti-Scottish: it took an English army
To settle the hash of that kilted butcher
Macbeth. He made jokes about the Welsh, the
French, the Danes, the Italians and the Spanish.
He accused a West Indian (or possibly Algerian)
Of trying to rape a white girl unsuccessfully.
If it wasn't a base Judean he displayed
As criminally careless with pearls, then
It was an equally base Indian. Thank God
He hadn't heard of the Australians!

To be sure, he was the servant of his public,
A rough unlettered lot, who rarely washed
And dwelt in the polluted alleys of London
Or the corners of slippery palaces. There wasn't
A drama critic of independent mind among them.
Even so, he must bear most of the blame,
He could have stayed in Stratford and led a
Quiet and useful life.

Worst of all, he believed in good and evil,
And mixed them up in a deliberately nasty
And confusing way. A shifty character,
He pictured the human condition as one of
Unending and uneasy struggle, not to be
Resolved in a *haiku* or even a television
Debate. He made difficulties, he made
Much ado about nothing.

Now that we've stripped him clean
Of his poetry, we can see him plain.
Plainly he'll have to go.

D J ENRIGHT (1973)

To poison plays, I see some where they sit,
Scattered, like ratsbane, up and down the pit.

WILLIAM CONGREVE (1697)

By Deputy

As Shakespeare could not write his plays
   (If Mrs Gallup's not mistaken),
I think how wise in many ways
   He was to have them done by Bacon;
They might have mouldered on the shelf,
   Mere minor dramas (and he knew it!)
If he had written them himself
   Instead of letting Bacon do it.

ARTHUR ST JOHN ADCOCK (1903)

Shakespeare

Others abide our question. Thou art free.
We ask and ask – Thou smilest and art still,
Out-topping knowledge. For the loftiest hill,
Who to the stars uncrowns his majesty,

Planting his steadfast footsteps in the sea,
Making the heaven of heavens his dwelling-place,
Spares but the cloudy border of his base
To the foil'd searching of mortality;

And thou, who didst the stars and sunbeams know,
Self-school'd, self-scann'd, self-honour'd, self-secure,
Didst tread on earth unguess'd at. – Better so!

All pains the immortal spirit must endure,
All weakness which impairs, all griefs which bow,
Find their sole speech in that victorious brow.

MATTHEW ARNOLD (1844)

'A Posy Made of Weeds'
Prologue to *The Rehearsal*

We might well call this short mock-play of ours,
A posy made of weeds instead of flowers;
Yet such have been presented to your noses,
And there are such, I fear, who thought 'em roses.
Would some of 'em were here, to see, this night,
What stuff it is in which they took delight.

Here brisk insipid rogues, for wit, let fall
Sometimes dull sense; but oft'ner none at all.
There, strutting heroes, with a grim-fac'd train,
Shall brave the gods, in King Cambyses' vein.
For (changing rules, of late, as if man writ
In spite of reason, nature, art and wit)
Our poets make us laugh at tragedy,
And with their comedies they make us cry.

Now critics, do your worst, that here are met;
For, like a rook, I have hedg'd in my bet.
If you approve, I shall assume the state
Of those high-flyers whom I imitate:
And justly too, for I will teach you more
Than ever they would let you know before.
I will not only show the feats they do,
But give you all their reasons for 'em too.

Some honour may to me from hence arise;
But if, by my endeavours you grow wise,
And what you once so prais'd, shall now despise;
Then I'll cry out, swell'd with poetic rage,
'Tis I, John Lacy, have reform'd your stage.

GEORGE VILLIERS,
DUKE OF BUCKINGHAM (1671)

The Rehearsal is a devastating burlesque of the heroic drama preva-
lent in the Restoration period (with side-swipes at other genres), and
the main butt of its ridicule is Dryden himself, easily recognizable in
the leading character, said to have been played to the life by the
brilliant John Lacy (d 1681).

'Eavesdropping'

From *An Essay on Poetry*

First, then, soliloquies had need be few,
Extremely short, and spoke in passion too.
Our lovers talking to themselves, for want
Of others, make the pit their confidant;
Nor is the matter mended yet, if thus
They trust a friend, only to tell it us.

JOHN SHEFFIELD, 1ST DUKE OF
BUCKINGHAM AND NORMANBY (1682)

'A Woman's Comedy'

Epilogue to *Sir Patient Fancy*, spoken by Nell Gwynn

MRS GWYNN (*looking about*):

I here and there o'erheard a coxcomb cry,
'Ah, rot it, 'tis a woman's comedy,
One, who because she lately chanced to please us,
With her damned stuff will never cease to tease us.'
What has poor woman done that she must be
Debarred from sense and sacred poetry?
Why in this age has Heaven allowed you more,
And woman less of wit than heretofore?

We once were famed in story, and could write
Equal to men; could govern, nay, could fight.
We still have passive valour, and can show,
Would custom give us leave, the active too,
Since we no provocations want from you.

For who but we could your dull fopperies bear,
Your saucy love and your brisk nonsense hear;
Endure your worse than womanish affectation,
Which renders you the nuisance of the nation;
Scorned even by all the misses of the town,
A jest to vizard mask and pit-buffoon;
A glass by which the admiring country fool
May learn to dress himself *en ridicule*,
Both striving who shall most ingenious grow
In lewdness, foppery, nonsense, noise and show.

And yet to these fine things we must submit
Our reason, arms, our laurels and our wit.
Because we do not laugh at you when lewd,
And scorn and cudgel ye when you are rude,
That we have nobler souls than you we prove,
By how much more we're sensible of love;
Quickest in finding all the subtlest ways
To make your joys, why not to make you plays?
We best can find your foibles, know our own,
And jilts and cuckolds now best please the town;
Your way of writing's out of fashion grown.
Method and rule you only understand –
Pursue that way of fooling and be damned.
Your learned cant of action, time and place
Must all give way to the unlaboured farce.
To all the men of wit we will subscribe
But for your half-wits, you unthinking tribe,
We'll let you see, whate'er besides we do,
How artfully we copy some of you:
And if you're drawn to th' life, pray tell me then,
Why women should not write as well as men?

APHRA BEHN (1678)

'The Pain of Thinking'

Epilogue to *The Sister,* by Mrs Charlotte Lennox

What! Five long acts – and all to make us wiser!
Our authoress sure has wanted an adviser.
Had she consulted *me,* she should have made
Her moral play a speaking masquerade;
Warm'd up each bustling scene, and in her rage
Have emptied all the green-room on the stage.
My life on 't, this had kept her play from sinking,
Have pleas'd our eyes, and sav'd the pain of thinking.

OLIVER GOLDSMITH (1769)

'Epilogues'

Could poets but foresee how plays would take,
Then they could tell what epilogues to make.

WILLIAM CONGREVE (1694)

'Mongst all the rules the ancients had in vogue,
We find no mention of an epilogue,
Which plainly shows they're innovations, brought
Since rules, design, and nature were forgot.

COLLEY CIBBER (1702)

The ancient epilogue, as critics write,
Was, clap your hands, excuse us, and good-night.

JOHN GAY (1717)

Impromptu Epitaph

Here lies Nolly Goldsmith, for shortness call'd Noll,
Who wrote like an angel, but talk'd like poor Poll.

DAVID GARRICK (1774)

'*Incongruous Mongrel*'
From *The Thespiad*

Sure, of all monsters bred in Poet's brain,
When hot meat makes him venturesome and vain,
Compelling him to write or else to burst –
Some dappled melodrame is most accurst.
Incongruous mongrel! And misshapen o'er,
With all that ever shamed the stage before:
Drum, trumpet, thunder, rosin, painted tin,
A storm, a song, a battle, and a grin.
Men, to make waves, a verdant carpet kick,
And even old Neptune never smells the trick.
Till to delight the heart, and wring the soul,
A murder and a marriage crown the whole.

ANON (1809)

Give us Lightning and Thunder, Flames, Daggers and Rage;
With events that ne'er happened, except on the Stage;
When your Spectre departs, through a trapdoor ingulph
    her,
Burn under her nose, too, some brimstone and sulpher.

M G LEWIS (1798)

Curtain!

Villain shows his indiscretion;
Villain's partner makes confession;
Juvenile with golden tresses
Finds her pa, and dons long dresses;
Scapegrace comes home, money-laiden;
Hero comforts tearful maiden;
Soubrette marries loyal chappie;
Villain skips, and all are happy.

PAUL LAURENCE DUNBAR (1895)

Through all the drama – whether damn'd or not –
Love gilds the scene, and women guide the plot.

RICHARD BRINSLEY SHERIDAN (1775)

In the Good Old Days

A Song

In the good old days, in those costume plays,
    When a song was call'd a lay, sir,
When they played high jinks, and they said methinks,
    'Tis well, alack a day sir!
Out! varlet out! thou 'rt a clumsy lout!
    Ha! sayest thou, thou wilt, sir?
Split me! Zounds! Odd's blood! Thou shalt chew the cud!
    Have at thee in friendly tilt, sir!

To say they never swore in the good old days of yore,
    Would be highly incorrect, sir;
They heartily abused one another when they used
    The words that I select, sir.

In those good old days, in those costume plays,
    They'd carry on a dispute in
Language most polite; though we moderns might
    Consider it high falutin!
'Thou should'st feel the weight, on that ugly pate
    Of my trusty Toledo blade, sir!
But I would not hurt such a malapert
Nay! beshrew me! I'm not afraid, sir!'

    To say they never swore, &c.

In those good old days, in those dear old days,
    When folks would say, 'I ween,' sir,
By my troth, gad zooks! but I like thy looks,
    Thou hast a courtly mien, sir;
Pledge my true love's name by my knightly fame,
    Her eyes like stars do shine, sir,
Stap my vitals, sir; thou 'rt a mangy cur!
    Go to! thou 'rt flushed with wine, sir!

    To say they never swore, &c.

CHARLES INGLE (1894)

Funny Without Being Vulgar

From a Song

I once took a part in a beautiful play,
    Which was funny without being vulgar.
The piece was produced at a gay matinée,
    It was funny without being vulgar.
'Twas not a success, I am bound to admit,
The only one person who did make a hit,
Was a gent with a brick at the back of the pit,
    He was funny without being vulgar.

HARRY BRETT (*c* 1890)

Chocolates

Once some people were visting Chekhov.
While they made remarks about his genius
the Master fidgeted. Finally
he said, 'Do you like chocolates?'

They were astonished, and silent.
He repeated the question,
whereupon one lady plucked up her courage
and murmured shyly, 'Yes.'

'Tell me,' he said, leaning forward,
light glinting from his spectacles,
'what kind? The light, sweet chocolate
or the dark, bitter kind?'

The conversation became general.
They spoke of cherry centres,
of almonds and Brazil nuts.
Losing their inhibitions
they interrupted one another.
For people may not know what they think
about politics in the Balkans,
or the vexed question of men and women,

but everyone has a definite opinion
about the flavour of shredded coconut.
Finally someone spoke of chocolates filled with liqueur,
and everyone, even the author of *Uncle Vanya*,
was at a loss for words.

As they were leaving he stood by the door
and took their hands.
              In the coach returning to Petersburg
they agreed that it had been a most
unusual conversation.

LOUIS SIMPSON (1980)

A Memory

When I was as high as that,
I saw a poet in his hat.
I think the poet must have smiled
At such a solemn gazing child.

Now isn't it a funny thing
To get a sight of J M Synge,
And notice nothing but his hat?
Yet life is often queer like that.

L A G STRONG (1923)

G is Galsworthy. We could do after all
with a little less worth and rather more gall.

HUMBERT WOLFE (1932)

O is O'Neill. The theatre was packed,
though a few may have died in the 49th act.

HUMBERT WOLFE (1932)

G B S – Ninety

After these ninety years, he can survey
Changes enough, so many due to him: –
Old wax-work melted down, old tinsel dim,
Old sentimental clock-work put away.

There the old playthings with their lovers lie;
But he remains, the bright mind ever young,
The glorious great heart, the witty tongue,
Erasing Shaw, who made the folly die.

Is there a cranny in our old conceit
Unlightened by the brightness of his mind?
Is there a blinker, making many blind,
Unrent by him, to show that light is sweet?

Is there a mystery in life or fate
To which his spirit has not sought a door?
Is there a play, in all his pungent store,
Not touching home? unlinked with something great?

Honour him living, all Earth's brightest brains.
Let Ministers of Fine Arts, centuries hence,
Order him statues; let us have more sense,
And call a splendour great while he remains.

JOHN MASEFIELD (1946)

J is for Shaw. As his dotage increases
he thinks himself Jupiter, Jahwe and Jesus.

HUMBERT WOLFE (1932)

Social Grace

I expect you've heard this a million times before
But I absolutely adored your last play
I went four times – and now to think
That here I am actually talking to you!
It's thrilling! Honestly it is, I mean,
It's always thrilling isn't it to meet someone really
   celebrated?
I mean someone who really does things.
I expect all this is a terrible bore for you.
After all you go everywhere and know everybody.
It must be wonderful to go absolutely everywhere
And know absolutely everybody and – Oh dear –
Then to have to listen to someone like me,
I mean someone absolutely ordinary just one of your public.
No one will believe me when I tell them
That I have actually been talking to the great man himself.
It must be wonderful to be so frightfully brainy
And know all the things that you know
I'm not brainy a bit, neither is my husband,
Just plain humdrum, that's what we are.
But we do come up to town occasionally
And go to shows and things. Actually my husband
Is quite a critic, not professionally of course,
What I mean is that he isn't all that easily pleased.
He doesn't like everything. Oh no not by any means.
He simply hated that thing at the Haymarket
Which everybody went on about. 'Rubbish' he said,
Straight out like that, 'Damned Rubbish!'
I nearly died because heaps of people were listening.
But that's quite typical of him. He just says what he thinks.
And he can't stand all this highbrow stuff –
Do you know what I mean? – All these plays about people
   being miserable
And never getting what they want and not even committing
   suicide

But just being absolutely wretched. He says he goes to the
    theatre
To have a good time. That's why he simply loves all your
    things,
    I mean they relax him and he doesn't have to think.
And he certainly does love a good laugh.
You should have seen him the other night when we went to
    that film
With what's-her-name in it – I can't remember the title.
I thought he'd have a fit, honestly I did.
You must know the one I mean, the one about the man
    who comes home
And finds his wife has been carrying on with his best friend
And of course he's furious at first and then he decides to
    teach her a lesson.
You must have seen it. I wish I could remember the name
But that's absolutely typical of me, I've got a head like a
    sieve,
I keep on forgetting things and as for names – well!
I just cannot for the life of me remember them.
Faces yes, I never forget a face because I happen to be
    naturally observant
And always have been since I was a tiny kiddie
But names – Oh dear! I'm quite hopeless.
I feel such a fool sometimes
I do honestly.

NOEL COWARD (1967)

N is for Noel. His genius is not
deep thinking, but thinking a little a lot.

HUMBERT WOLFE (1932)

The Critic

The critic of the morning Press
Devotes his day to idleness;
But then he has to sit and write
His notice very late at night,
When he would so much rather be
Tucked up in bed like you and me.
No wonder he's a trifle sharp
And shows a tendency to carp.

Captious and cross the critic creeps
Exhausted into bed and sleeps.
Rising next day in buoyant mood
He feels once more that life is good;
Springs out of bed and cuts a caper
And asks to see the morning paper.
His cheeks turn pale; his eyes grow wet;
He's filled with infinite regret,
As he peruses in the light
The brutal things he wrote last night.

GUY BOAS (1925)

Critics avaunt! For you are fish of prey,
And feed, like sharks, upon an infant play.

WILLIAM CONGREVE (1693)

ACTORS

Some time let gorgeous Tragedy
In scepter'd pall come sweeping by.

JOHN MILTON (1645)

The Theatrical Path

When first I began to talk big,
   I chose the theatrical path, sir;
I put on a tragedy wig,
   And flourished my dagger of lath, sir.
Love rais'd such a flame in my heart
   That I fancy it is not quite cool yet,
When in Romeo I strutted my part,
   And Shelah Granore was my Juliet.

Her lip was so prettily curl'd;
   Her heart than a turtle's was kinder;
But one day she walked out of the world,
   And left her poor Romeo behind her.
In despair at the cruel control
   Of fortune so fierce and so frisky,
I seiz'd on our tragedy bowl –
   And fill'd up a brimmer of whisky.

Says I, 'This shall finish all strife'
   (And my tears they fell faster and thicker),
'I'll soon put an end to my life –
   But I'll first put an end to my liquor.'
The curtain drew up for *Macbeth*:
   I paus'd between glory and sorrow –
Says I: 'I'm resolved upon death,
   But I'll just put it off till to-morrow.'

THOMAS LOVE PEACOCK (*c* 1818)

Actors

From *The Play-House. A Satire*

To speak 'em all were tedious to discuss;
But if you'll lump 'em, they're exactly thus:
A pimping, sponging, idle, impious race,
The shame of virtue, and despair of grace;
A nest of lechers worse than Sodom bore,
And justly merit to be punish'd more;
Diseas'd, in debt, and ev'ry moment dunn'd,
By all good Christians loath'd, and their own kindred
    shunn'd.
To say more of 'em would be wasting time,
For it with justice may be thought a crime
To let such rubbish have a place in rhyme.

ROBERT GOULD (1709)

We may be pelted off for ought we know
With apples, eggs, or stones, from thence below.

ROBERT TAILOR (1613)

Portrayal of Past and Present in One

Whatever you portray you should always portray
As if it were happening now. Engrossed
The silent crowd sits in the darkness, lured
Away from its routine affairs. Now
The fisherman's wife is being brought her son whom
The generals have killed. Even what has just happened
In her room is wiped out. What is happening here is
Happening now and just the once. To act in this way
Is habitual with you, and now I am advising you
To ally this habit with yet another: that is, that your acting
    should

At the same time express the fact that this instant
On your stage is often repeated; only yesterday
You were acting it, and tomorrow too
Given spectactors, there will be a further performance.
Nor should you let the Now blot out the
Previously and Afterwards, nor for that matter whatever
Is even now happening outside the theatre and is similar in
   kind
Nor even things that have nothing to do with it all – none
   of this
Should you allow to be entirely forgotten.
So you should simply make the instant
Stand out, without in the process hiding
What you are making it stand out from. Give your acting
That progression of one-thing-after-another, that attitude of
Working up what you have taken on. In this way
You will show the flow of events and also the course
Of your work, permitting the spectator
To experience this Now on many levels, coming from
   Previously and
Merging into Afterwards, also having much else now
Alongside it. He is sitting not only
In your theatre but also
In the world.

BERTOLT BRECHT (1938)
(Trans. John Willett)

   . . . to show
Things never done, with that true life
That thoughts and wits should stand at strife
Whether the things now shown be true,
Or whether we ourselves now do
The things we but present.

LORDING BARRY (1608)

'The Mirror up to Nature'

From the Prologue to *Damon and Pithias*

In comedies, the greatest skill is this: rightly to touch
All things to the quick, and eke to frame each person so
That by his common talk you may his nature rightly know.
A roister ought not preach, that were too strange to hear,
But as from virtue he doth swerve so ought his words
    appear.
The old man is sober, the young man rash, the lover
    triumphing in joys,
The matron grave, the harlot wild and full of wanton toys.
Which all in one course they in no wise do agree:
So correspondent to their kind their speeches ought to be.
Which speeches well pronounced, with action lively framed,
If this offend the lookers on, let Horace then be blamed,
Which hath our author taught at school from whom he doth
    not swerve,
In all such kind of exercise decorum to observe.

RICHARD EDWARDS (1565)

'The Motive and the Cue for Passion'

From *Hamlet*, Act Two, Scene II

O, what a rogue and peasant slave am I!
Is it not monstrous that this player here,
But in a fiction, in a dream of passion,
Could force his soul so to his own conceit
That from her working all his visage wann'd;
Tears in his eyes, distraction in's aspect,
A broken voice, and his whole function suiting
With forms to his conceit? And all for nothing!
For Hecuba!
What's Hecuba to him or he to Hecuba,
That he should weep for her? What would he do,

Had he the motive and the cue for passion
That I have? He would drown the stage with tears,
And cleave the general ear with horrid speech;
Make mad the guilty, and appal the free,
Confound the ignorant, and amaze indeed
The very faculties of eyes and ears.

WILLIAM SHAKESPEARE (*c* 1600)

'The Actors are at Hand'

From *A Midsummer Night's Dream*, Act Five, Scene I

Enter, with a Trumpet *before them, as in dumb show,* PYRAMUS
and THISBY, WALL, MOONSHINE, *and* LION.

PROLOGUE   Gentles, perchance you wonder at this show;
But wonder on, till truth make all things plain.
This man is Pyramus, if you would know;
This beauteous lady Thisby is certain.
This man, with lime and rough-cast, doth
    present
Wall, that vile Wall which did these lovers
    sunder;
And through Wall's chink, poor souls, they are
    content
To whisper. At the which let no man wonder.
This man, with lanthorn, dog, and bush of
    thorn,
Presenteth Moonshine; for, if you will know,
By moonshine did these lovers think no scorn
To meet at Ninus' tomb, there, there to woo.
This grisly beast, which Lion hight by name,
The trusty Thisby, coming first by night,
Did scare away, or rather did affright;
And as she fled, her mantle she did fall;
Which Lion vile with bloody mouth did stain.
Anon comes Pyramus, sweet youth and tall,
And finds his trusty Thisby's mantle slain;

Whereat with blade, with bloody blameful
   blade,
He bravely broach'd his boiling bloody breast;
And Thisby, tarrying in mulberry shade,
His dagger drew, and died. For all the rest,
Let Lion, Moonshine, wall and lovers twain,
At large discourse while here they do remain.

           WILLIAM SHAKESPEARE (*c* 1595)

When Burbage Played

When Burbage played, the stage was bare
Of fount and temple, tower and stair.
Two broadswords eked a battle out;
Two supers made a rabble rout;
The Throne of Denmark was a chair!

And yet, no less the audience there
Thrilled through all changes of Despair,
Hope, Anger, Fear, Delight and Doubt,
    When Burbage played.

This is the Actor's gift; to share
All moods, all passions, nor to care
One whit for scene, so he without
Can lead men's minds the roundabout,
Stirred as of old these hearers were
    When Burbage played.

           AUSTIN DOBSON (1937)

Richard Burbage (*c* 1567–1619), great English actor, and first player
of Shakespeare's tragic roles, survived Shakespeare by three years,
dying at the height of his powers. It has been said that, so closely was
he identified with Shakespeare's plays, men did not fully realize the
playwright was dead until Burbage himself died too.

On the death of that great Master

in his art and quality, painting and playing, R Burbage

Astronomers and Stargazers this year
Write but of four eclipses, five appear,
Death interposing Burbage and there staying
Hath made a veritable eclipse of playing.

THOMAS MIDDLETON (1619)

To make the weeper laugh, the laugher weep,
He had the dialect and different skill,
Catching all passions in his craft of will.

WILLIAM SHAKESPEARE (1609)

Elegy

on the death of the famous actor R Burbage

He's gone, and with him what a world is dead
Which he revived, to be renewed so
No more. Young Hamlet, old Hieronimo,
Kind Lear, the grieved Moor, and more beside
That lived in him, have now for ever died.

Oft have I seen him leap into a grave
Suiting the person, which he seemed to have,
Of a sad lover, with so true an eye
That then I would have sworn he meant to die;
Oft have I seen him play his part in jest,
So lively, that spectators, and the rest
Of his sad crew, while he seemed to bleed
Amazed thought that he had died indeed.
Oh! Did not knowledge check me, I should swear
Even yet it is a false report I hear,

And think that he who did so truly feign
Is only dead in jest to live again.
But now this part he acts, not plays; 'tis known
Others he played, but now he acts his own.

England's great Roscius, for what Roscius
Was more to Rome than Burbage was to us?
How to the person did he suit his face,
How did his speech become him, and his face
Suit with his speech, whilst not a word did fall
Without just weight to balance it withal. . . .

Poets! Whose glory 'twas of late to hear
Your lines so well exprest: henceforth forebear
And write no more, or if you do 't, let 't be
In comic scenes, for tragic parts you see
Die all with him; nay, rather sluice your eyes
And henceforth write naught else but tragedies. . . .

And you, his sad companions, to whom Lent
Becomes more lenten in this accident,
Henceforth your wavering flag no more hang out.
Play now no more at all; when round about
We look and miss the Atlas of the sphere
What comfort think you have we to be there?
And how can you delight in playing when
Sad mourning so affecteth other men?

ANON (1619)

Edward Alleyn

If Rome so great, and in her wisest age,
Fear'd not to boast the glories of her stage,
As skilful Roscius and grave Æsop, men,
Yet crown'd with honours as with riches then;

Who had no less a trumpet of their name
Than Cicero, whose every breath was fame;
How can so great example die in me,
That, Alleyn, I should pause to publish thee?
Who both their graces in thyself hast more
Outstript, than they did all that went before;
And present worth in all dost so contract,
As others speak, but only thou dost act.
Wear this renown: 'tis just, that who did give
So many poets life, by one should live.

BEN JONSON (1616)

Edward Alleyn (1566–1626) was the contemporary and only peer of
Richard Burbage on the Elizabethan stage. He joined Henslowe's
management at the newly opened Rose Theatre, where he made a
great reputation for himself, particularly in Marlowe's plays. He was
in due course prosperous enough to retire to Dulwich, where he
founded a hospital and school known as the College of God's Gift,
now Dulwich College.

The gull gets on a surplice,
    With a cross upon his breast,
Like Alleyn playing Faustus,
    In that manner he was dressed.

SAMUEL ROWLANDS (1609)

Richard Tarleton

A poem with a portrait

The picture here set down
    Within this letter T,
Aright doth show the form and shape
    Of Tarleton unto thee.

When he in pleasant wise
   The Counterfeit exprest
Of Clown with coat of russet hue
   And start-ups with the rest.

Who merry many made
   When he appeared in sight,
The grave and wise as well as rude
   At him did take delight.

The party now is gone
   And closely clad in clay,
Of all the Jesters in the land
   He bare the praise away.

Now hath he played his part
   And sure he is of this,
If he in Christ did die, to live
   With him in lasting bliss.

ANON (*c* 1588)

Richard Tarleton (*d* 1588), pre-eminent Elizabethan clown, was probably the original of the jester Yorick, whom Hamlet fondly mourned. When he died Edmund Spenser wrote that with him 'all joy and jolly merriment is also deaded.'

Tarleton when his head was only seen,
The tire-house door and tapestry between,
Set all the multitude in such a laughter,
They could not hold for scarce an hour after.

HENRY PEACHAM (1620)

On Salathiel Pavy

A child of Queen Elizabeth's Chapel

Weep with me, all you that read
This little story;
And know, for whom a tear you shed
Death's self is sorry.
'Twas a child that so did thrive
In grace and feature,
As Heaven and Nature seemed to strive
Which owned the creature.
Years he numbered scarce thirteen
When Fates turned cruel,
Yet three filled Zodiacs had he been
The Stage's jewel;
And did act (what now we moan)
Old men so duly
As sooth the Parcae thought him one,
He played so truly.
So, by error, to his fate
They all consented;
But, viewing him since, alas, too late!
They have repented;
And have sought, to give new birth,
In baths to steep him;
But, being so much too good for earth,
Heaven vows to keep him.

BEN JONSON (1603)

Salathiel Pavy (1590–1603) was a member of the foremost of the companies of boy-players which had developed during the sixteenth century. As Shakespeare makes Rosencrantz tell Hamlet, 'they berattle the common stages' and 'there has been much ado on both sides.'

'The First Actress'

A Prologue, to introduce the first woman that came to act on the stage, in the tragedy called The Moor of Venice

I come, unknown to any of the rest,
To tell you news; I saw the lady drest:
The woman plays to-day: mistake me not,
No man in gown, or page in petticoat:
A woman to my knowledge; yet I can't,
If I should die, make affidavit on't.

Do you not twitter, gentlemen? I know
You will be censuring: do it fairly though.
'Tis *possible* a virtuous woman may
Abhor all sorts of looseness, and yet play;
Play on the stage, – where all eyes are upon her: –
Shall we count that a crime, France counts an honour?

In other kingdoms husbands safely trust 'em;
The difference lies only in the custom.
And let it be our custom, I advise;
I'm sure this custom's better than th' excise,
And may procure *us* custom: hearts of flint
Will melt in passion, when a woman's in't.

But gentlemen, you that as judges sit
In the star-chamber of the house, the pit,
Have modest thoughts of her; pray, do not run
To give her visits when the play is done,
With '*damn me, your most humble servant, lady*;'
She knows these things as well as you, it may be:
Not a bit there, dear gallants, she doth know
Her own deserts – and your temptations too –

But to the point: – In this reforming age
We have intents to civilize the stage.
Our women are defective, and so siz'd,
You'd think they were some of the guard disguis'd:
For, to speak truth, men act, that are between
Forty and fifty, wenches of fifteen;
With bone so large, and nerve so incompliant,
When you call Desdemona, enter Giant –

We shall purge every thing that is unclean,
Lascivious, scurrilous, impious, or obscene;
And when we've put all things in this fair way,
Barebones himself may come to see a play.

THOMAS JORDAN (1660)

Traditionally, only men had ever played on the English stage, and, even after Charles II had brought in the French fashion of using women for female parts, the old custom still often prevailed. One of the last of the boy-actors to play women was Edward Kynaston (c 1640–1706). Pepys wrote, 'He made the loveliest lady that I ever saw,' and it is on record that fine ladies used to like being seen driving with him in his stage dress in the park after the play.

Prologue

to the Reviv'd Alchemist

The *Alchemist*: fire, breeding gold, our theme;
Here must no melancholy be, nor phlegm.
Young Ben, not Old, writ this, when in his prime,
Solid in judgement, and in wit sublime.

The Sisters who at Thespian Springs their blood
Cool with fresh streams, all, in a merry mood,
Their wat'ry cups and pittances declin'd,
At Bread Street's Mermaid with our Poet din'd;
Where, what they drank, or who play'd most the rig,
Fame modestly conceals: but he grew big
Of this priz'd issue; when a jovial maid,
His brows besprinkling with Canary, said:

Pregnant by us, produce no mortal birth;
Thy active soul, quitting the sordid earth,
Shall 'mongst Heav'n's glitt'ring hieroglyphics trade,
And Pegasus, our winged sumpter, jade,
Who from Parnassus never brought to Greece,
Nor Roman stage, so rare a masterpiece.

This story, true or false, may well be spar'd;
The Actors are in question, not the Bard:
How they shall humour their oft-varied parts,
To get your money, company, and hearts,
Since all tradition and like helps are lost.

Reading our Bill new pasted on the post,
Grave stagers both, one, to the other said,
THE *Alchemist*? What! Are the fellows mad?
Who shall Doll Common act? Their tender tibs
Have neither lungs, nor confidence, nor ribs.

Who Face, and Subtle? Parts, all air, and fire:
They whom the Author did himself inspire,
Taught, line by line, each tittle, accent, word,
Ne'er reached his height; all after, more absurd,
Shadows of fainter shadows, wheresoe'er
A Fox he pencill'd, copied out a Bear.

Encouragement for young beginners small;
Yet howsoe'er we'll venture; have at All.
Bold ignorance, they say, falls seldom short
In camp, the country, city, or the court.

Arm'd with the influence of your fair aspects,
Our selves we'll conquer, and our own defects,
A thousand eyes dart rays into our hearts,
Would make stones speak, and stocks play well their parts:
Some few malignant beams we need not fear,
Where shines such glory in so bright a sphere.

ANON (*c* 1660)

After eighteen years of virtual suppression of the public theatres
under the Commonwealth, it was hard for both players and playgoers to pick up where they had left off. This prologue sums up the
doubts of many about the adequacy of a new generation of actors and
the new-fangled custom of women ('tender tibs') in raucous parts
like Doll Common.

'These Our Actors'

I'd have a play could I but to my mind
Good actors get, but that's not now to find,
For, oh, th' are dead, this age affordeth none,
Good actors all long since are dead and gone.

WILLIAM GODDARD (1615)

As in a play scenes vary by degrees,
And, though the various prospects change, they please;
So, when a band of ancient actors die,
Another set the theatres supply.

An Essay on the Theatres (*c* 1660)

Nell Gwynn

The orange-basket her fair arm did suit,
Laden with pippins and Hesperian fruit;
This first step raised, to the wond'ring pit she sold
The lovely fruit, smiling with streaks of gold.
Fate now for her did its whole force engage,
And from the pit she mounted to the stage;
There in full lustre did her glories shine,
And long eclips'd spread forth their light divine;
There Hart and Rowley's soul she did ensnare,
And make a King rival to a Play'r.

Attributed to
JOHN WILMOT, EARL OF ROCHESTER (*c* 1670)

'Nelly's Ghost'

Epilogue to *Tyrannic Love, or The Royal Martyr*,
spoken by Mrs Ellen Gwynn when she was to be
carried off dead by the Bearers

(*To the Bearer:*)

Hold! Are you mad? You damned, confounded dog!
I am to rise, and speak the epilogue.

(*To the Audience:*)

I come, kind gentlemen, strange news to tell ye;
I am the ghost of poor departed Nelly.
Sweet ladies, be not frighted; I'll be civil;
I'm what I was, a little harmless devil.
For, after death, we sprites have just such natures,
We had, for all the world, when human creatures;
And, therefore, I, that was an actress here,
Play all my tricks in hell, a goblin there.
Gallants, look to 't, you say there are no sprites;
But I'll come dance about your beds at nights;

And faith you'll be in a sweet kind of taking,
When I surprise you between sleep and waking.
To tell you true, I walk, because I die
Out of my calling, in a tragedy.
O poet, damned dull poet, who could prove
So senseless, to make Nelly die for love!
Nay, what's yet worse, to kill me in the prime
Of Easter–term, in tart and cheese–cake time!
I'll fit the fop; for I'll not one word say,
To excuse his godly, out–of–fashion play;
A play, which, if you dare but twice sit out,
You'll all be slandered, and be thought devout.
But, farewell, gentlemen, make haste to me,
I'm sure ere long to have your company.
As for my epitaph when I am gone,
I'll trust no poet, but will write my own:-

Here Nelly lies, who, though she lived a slattern,
Yet died a princess, acting in St Catherine.

JOHN DRYDEN (1669)

'Actors are to Seem'

From *An Essay on the Theatres, or the Art of Acting*

All actors are to seem what they are not;
Which to perform, themselves must be forgot;
Their mind must lost in character be shown,
Nor once betray a passion of their own:
Must to the business of the stage attend
And height of action with their silence blend:
Or in the front, aside or back retired,
Something to do, or seem, is still required:
This common rule should practised be by all
From Jobson chaunting in the cobbler's stall,
To Caesar thund'ring in the Capitol,

'Tis not enough if you can catch the cue,
A strict attention's to the audience due;
Gaze not around on them; they do not pay
To see you turn spectators, but to play.
If you are curious, there are other means,
From the looped curtains, or behind the scenes. . . .

'Tis said, as actors on the stage make known
All others' foibles, nor reveal their own,
Many there are who've sat out many a play
Nor went near the twelfth hour fatigued away;
Who on the stage the players have admired,
Have wished to know their humours when retired:
They of strange things behind the curtain hear,
And wonder what those famous Green Rooms are.

For Fame says, many go behind the scenes,
To romp with goddesses and joke with queens.
With half drunk bishops talk of smutty things,
Bow'd to by emperors and shook hands by kings.

ANON (c 1660)

An added attraction in the Green Room, after the Restoration had
unleashed women onto the stage, was the frequent presence of
actresses playing breeches parts – leading parts written for men but
played by women. The fashion never quite lost its hold and still
lingers on with the Principal Boy in pantomime.

'Breeches Parts'

As Woman let me with the Men prevail,
And with the Ladies as I look like Male.
'Tis worth your money that such legs appear;
These are not to be seen so cheap elsewhere:
In short, commend this play, or by this light,
We will not sup with one of you tonight.

JOHN CORYE (1672)

Oh, would the higher powers be kind to us;
And grant us to set up a female house!
We'll make ourselves to please both sexes then,
To the men women, to the women men.
Here, we presume, our legs are no ill sight.
And they will give you no ill dreams at night.
In dreams both sexes must their passion ease,
You make us then as civil as you please.

JOHN DRYDEN (1672)

When well form'd Harlow's seen in breeches
Her dainty leg the eye bewitches.

THOMAS BELLAMY (1795)

The Actor

A Poetical Epistle to Bonnell Thornton, Esq.

Acting, dear Thornton, its perfection draws,
From no observance of mechanic laws:
No settled maxims of a favourite stage,
No rules delivered down from age to age,
Let players nicely mark them as they will,
Can e'er entail hereditary skill.
If, 'mongst the humble hearers of the pit,
Some curious veteran critic chance to sit,
Is he pleased more because 'twas acted so
By Booth and Cibber thirty years ago?

The mind recalls an object held more dear,
And hates the copy, that it comes so near.
Why loved he Wilks's air, Booth's nervous tone?
In them 'twas natural, 'twas all their own.
A Garrick's genius must our wonder raise,
But gives his mimic no reflected praise. . . .

Perfection's top, with weary toil and pain,
'Tis genius only that can hope to gain.
The player's profession (though I hate the phrase,
'Tis so *mechanic* in these modern days)
Lies not in trick, or attitude, or start,
Nature's true knowledge is the only art.
The strong-felt passion bolts into his face,
The mind untouched, what is it but grimace!
To this one standard make your just appeal,
Here lies the golden secret; learn to *feel*.
Or fool, or monarch, happy, or distressed,
No actor pleases that is not *possessed*. . . .

Unskilful actors, like your mimic apes,
Will writhe their bodies in a thousand shapes;
However foreign from the poet's art,
No tragic hero but admires a start.
What though unfeeling of the nervous line,
Who but allows his *Attitude* is fine?
While a whole minute equipois'd he stands,
Till praise dismiss him with her echoing hands.
Resolv'd, though Nature hate the tedious pause,
By perseverance to extort applause.
When Romeo sorrowing at his Juliet's doom,
With eager madness bursts the canvas tomb,
The sudden whirl, stretch'd leg, and lifted staff,
Which please the vulgar, make the critic laugh.

ROBERT LLOYD (1760)

'That Pithy Lecture'

From *The Prompter*

The true perfection of your art to reach
No master guides you, nor no maxims teach.
Yet some there are who doubtless may explain,
The player's province through the drama's scene:
Churchill, I grant you, sense with sound unites,
His hints improve you, while his wit delights;
Of Lloyd's terse poem, treasure ev'ry line,
There rhyme and reason all their force combine;
But strike that pithy lecture to your heart,
Which Hamlet gives you for the actor's art;
The point of all that's written on the stage,
Is here comprised in Shakespeare's single page.

ANON (1810)

Kitty Clive

Here liv'd the laughter loving dame –
A matchless actress, Clive her name;
The Comic Muse with her retir'd,
And shed a tear when she expir'd.

HORACE WALPOLE (1774)

Henry Mossop

From *The Rosciad*

Mossop, attach'd to military plan,
Still kept his eye fixed on his right-hand man;
Whilst the mouth measures words with seeming skill
The right hand labours, and the left lies still.
For he resolv'd on scripture-grounds to go,
What the right doth, the left hand shall not know.

With studied impropriety of speech,
He soars beyond the hackney critic's reach;
To epithets allots emphatic state,
Whilst principals, ungrac'd, like lackies wait;
In ways first trodden by himself excels,
And stands alone in indeclinables;
Conjunction, preposition, adverb, join
To stamp new vigour in the nervous line;
In monosyllables his thunders roll,
HE, SHE, IT, and WE, YE, THEY, fright the soul.

CHARLES CHURCHILL (1763)

Tut, I can counterfeit the deep tragedian;
Speak and look back, and pry on every side,
Tremble and start at wagging of a straw,
Intending deep suspicion. Ghastly looks
Are at my service, like enforced smiles.

WILLIAM SHAKESPEARE (*c* 1592)

Nature few actors for themselves explore,
They copy those who copied her before.

The Prompter (1810)

Garrick and Shakespeare
From *The Task*

Man praises man; and Garrick's mem'ry next,
When time hath somewhat mellow'd it, and made
The idol of our worship while he liv'd
The god of our idolatry once more,
Shall have its altar; and the world shall go
In pilgrimage to bow before his shrine.

136

The theatre, too small, shall suffocate
Its squeez'd contents, and more than it admits
Shall sigh at their exclusion, and return
Ungratified. For there some noble lord
Shall stuff his shoulders with King Richard's bunch,
Or wrap himself in Hamlet's inky cloak,
And strut, and storm, and straddle, stamp, and stare,
To show the world how Garrick did not act –
For Garrick was a worshipper himself;
He drew the liturgy, and fram'd the rites
And solemn ceremonial of the day,
And call'd the world to worship on the banks
Of Avon, fam'd in song.

WILLIAM COWPER (1784)

David Garrick (1717–79) was one of the greatest of English actors, who brought about a revolutionary change in the established formal and declamatory style of delivery, introducing an expressive, mobile and eloquent interpretation of his parts. In 1769 he organised a great Shakespeare Jubilee at Stratford, though to some critical observers it seemed a celebration of the actor rather than the bard. It was also partly washed out by torrential rain.

Garrick

From *Retaliation*

Here lies David Garrick, describe him who can,
An abridgement of all that was pleasant in man:
As an actor, confess'd without rival to shine;
As a wit, if not first, in the very first line:
Yet, with talents like these, and an excellent heart,
This man had his failings – a dupe to his art.
Like an ill judging beauty, his colours he spread,
And be-plaster'd with rouge his own natural red.
On the stage he was natural, simple, affecting;
'Twas only that when he was off he was acting.

With no reason on earth to go out of his way,
He turn'd and he varied full ten times a day:
Though secure of our hearts, yet confoundedly sick
If they were not his own by finessing and trick:
He cast off his friends, as a huntsman his pack,
For he knew when he pleased he could whistle them back.
Of praise a mere glutton, he swallow'd what came,
And the puff of a dunce he mistook it for fame;
Till his relish grown callous, almost to disease,
Who pepper'd the highest was surest to please. . . .

But peace to his spirit, wherever it flies,
To act as an angel and mix with the skies:
Those poets, who owe their best fame to his skill
Shall still be his flatterers, go where he will;
Old Shakespeare receive him with praise and with love.
And Beaumonts and Bens be his Kellys above.

OLIVER GOLDSMITH (1774)

The story goes that, in the course of a convivial evening at the St James's Coffee House, a group of friends composed mock epitaphs on one another. Garrick contributed the well-known couplet on the playwright Oliver Goldsmith (see page 103), to which this is Goldsmith's reply, contained in his *Retaliation* on the whole lot of them.

'Harlequin Actor'

Epilogue to *She Stoops to Conquer*, written for Mr Lee Lewes

Hold! Prompter, hold! A word before your nonsense;
I'd speak a word or two to ease my conscience.
My pride forbids it ever should be said,
My heels eclips'd the honours of my head;
That I found humour in a piebald vest,
Or ever thought that jumping was a jest.

(*Takes off his mask.*)

Whence, and what art thou, visionary birth?
Nature disowns, and reason scorns thy mirth,
In thy black aspect every passion sleeps,
The joy that dimples, and the woe that weeps.
How hast thou fill'd the scene with all thy brood,
Of fools pursuing, and of fools pursu'd!
Whose ins and outs no ray of sense discloses,
Whose only plot it is to break our noses;
Whilst from below the trap-door Demons rise,
And from above the dangling deities;
And shall I mix in this unhallow'd crew?
May rosin'd lightning blast me, if I do!

No – I will act, I'll vindicate the stage;
Shakespeare himself shall feel my tragic rage.
Off! off! Vile trappings! A new passion reigns!
The madd'ning monarch revels in my veins.
Oh! For a Richard's voice to catch the theme:
'Give me another horse! Bind up my wounds! Soft – 'twas
    but a dream.'
Ay, 'twas but a dream, for now there's no retreating:
If I cease Harlequin, I cease from eating.

OLIVER GOLDSMITH (1773)

Before his appearance in this play, Charles Lee Lewes (1740–1803) had been specializing in playing the part of Harlequin. So it was daring of Goldsmith to cast him in the leading role of Young Marlow in his new comedy, *She Stoops to Conquer*. It was a great success, however, and the grateful author wrote this epilogue for him on the occasion of his Benefit on 7 May 1773. A Benefit was an occasional performance of which the takings (usually after deduction of management expenses) went to the individual actor as a means of supplementing his regular share or salary – usually inadequate. The Benefit might be an annual or seasonal occurrence, or might mark a special event, such as retirement, or be a means of help for an actor or his family in misfortune. Benefits were also held for more general charitable purposes.

Dorothy Jordan

Sportive Jordan, in thy smiles,
Love exhibits all its wiles:
Sprightly humour, native ease,
Such as thine must ever please.
Arch thy glance, bewitching fair;
Wildly floats thy graceful hair;
A child more favoured, more *alone*,
Euphrosyne shall never own.
Still charm as erst in all thy varied parts;
Still reign, deserving nymph, the queen of hearts;
For public merit private work combine,
To form th' unfading wreath so truly thine.

THOMAS BELLAMY (1795)

Mrs Jordan (1761–1816) was a gifted comedienne, especially noted
for her high-spirited performances as hoydens and in breeches parts.
Her affections led her into a number of liaisons, of which the most
notable was that with the Duke of Clarence, later William IV, whose
mistress she was for some years. She bore him ten children, while
continuing to act.

John Philip Kemble

From *The Thespiad*

Precise in passion, cautious ev'n in rage,
Lo! Kemble comes, the Euclid of the stage;
Who moves in given angles, squares a start,
And blows his Roman beak by rules of art;
Writhes with a grace to agony unknown,
And gallops half an octave in a groan.
His solemn voice, like death-bell heard afar,
Or death-watch clicking in an old crackt jar,
He measures out, monotonous and slow,
In-one-dull-long-sing-song-to-joy-or-woe.

The stoic sameness nothing can remove;
Nor will his rigid ham-strings bend to love.
John Kemble see you in all parts you will,
Lear, Romeo, Richard – 'tis John Kemble still.

ANON (1809)

J P Kemble (1757–1823) and his sister Sarah Siddons (1755–1831) were the most famous members of a notable theatrical family. He became very unpopular with the public when, as manager of the rebuilt Covent Garden Theatre after the fire of 1808, he raised the prices of admittance, thus causing the notorious OP (Old Prices) riots.

Mrs Siddons

From *Thoughts on Being Alone after Dinner*

'Tis, let me see, full sixteen years,
And wondrous short the time appears,
Since, with enquiry warm,
With beauty's novel power amazed,
I follow'd, midst the crowd, and gazed
On Siddons' beauteous form.

Up Bath's fatiguing streets I ran,
Just half pretending to be man,
And fearful to intrude;
Busied I looked on some employ,
Or limp'd to see some other boy,
Lest she should think me rude.

The sun was bright, and on her face,
As proud to show the stranger grace,
Shone with its purest rays;
And through the folds that veil'd her form,
Motion displayed its happiest charm,
To catch the admiring gaze.

The smiling lustre of her eyes,
That triumph'd in our wild surprise,
Well I remember still:
They spoke of joy to yield delight,
And plainly said, 'If I'm the sight,
Good people, take your fill.'

SIR THOMAS LAWRENCE (*c* 1798)

These verses by the portrait painter, Lawrence, recall the Sarah Siddons of her provincial days, before she had made her mark in London. Lawrence, like Gainsborough, Reynolds, and other artists of the time, painted several portraits of her.

Siddons

As when a child on some long winter's night,
Affrighted, clinging to its grandame's knees,
With eager wondering and perturb'd delight
Listens strange tales of fearful dark decrees
Mutter'd to wretch by necromantic spell;
Or of those hags, who, at the watching time
Of murky midnight, ride the air sublime,
And mingle foul embrace with fiends of hell,
Cold horror drinks its blood! Anon the tear
More gentle starts, to hear the beldame tell
Of pretty babes that lov'd each other dear,
Murder'd by cruel Uncle's mandate fell.
Ev'n such the shiv'ring joys thy tones impart,
Ev'n so thou, Siddons, meltest my sad heart.

SAMUEL TAYLOR COLERIDGE
and CHARLES LAMB (1794)

'Two Kinds of Vehicle'

From *The Thespiad*

The Poet tells us that in ancient days
Our ancestors in carts performed their plays.
Methinks the custom we might now renew,
And cart the gang of modern actors too.
Immortal Garrick, in an happier age,
Taught Sense to tread with Nature on the stage;
What poets wrote, mimetic play'rs displayed.
But now such narrow notions we condemn;
Bards study actors and not actors them.
To suit the play'r the drama is designed,
And Reynolds copies Munden, not mankind.

ANON (1809)

'Maudlin Old Stagers'

From *The Prompter*

What blind delusion or theatric rage,
Can keep that gang upon our fallen stage,
Of ragamuffins; who with scarcely brains
To stick the play-bills or to shift the scenes,
Persist to fret and strut their night along
In dull monotony and tame sing-song;
With rueful visage and a dismal whine,
Gravely burlesquing every classic line;
Maudlin old stagers, who beneath all praise,
Can no one feeling but compassion raise!

ANON (1810)

Edmund Kean

Thou art the sun's bright child!
The genius that irradiates thy mind,
Caught all its purity and light from heaven!
Thine is the task, with majesty most perfect,
To bind the passions captive in thy train;
Each crystal tear, that slumbers in the depth
Of feeling's fountain, doth obey thy call.
There's not a joy or sorrow mortals prove,
Or passion to humanity allied,
But tribute of allegiance owes to thee.
The shrine thou worshipest is nature's self,
The only altar genius deigns to seek.
Thine offering – a bold and burning mind,
Whose impulse guides thee to the realms of fame,
Where, crowned with well-earned laurels – all thine own –
I herald thee to immortality.

Attributed to GEORGE GORDON, LORD BYRON (c 1815)

This poem hails the genius of Edmund Kean (1787–1833), whose revolutionary performance of Shylock amazed London in 1814. 'To see him act,' said Coleridge, 'is like reading Shakespeare by flashes of lightning.' He had endured hard years as a strolling player before his London success, and continued to lead an erratic life. He finally collapsed during a performance of *Othello*, and died a few weeks later.

To W C Macready

*After his farewell performance, as Macbeth, at
Drury Lane, February 26, 1851*

Farewell, Macready, since tonight we part;
Full-handed thunders often have confessed
Thy power, well-used to move the public breast.
We thank thee with our voice, and from the heart.

Farewell, Macready, since this night we part.
Go, take thine honours home! Rank with the best,
Garrick and statelier Kemble, and the rest
Who made a nation purer through their art,
Thine is it that our drama did not die,
Nor flicker down to brainless pantomime,
And those gilt gauds men-children swarm to see.
Farewell, Macready; moral, grave, sublime,
Our Shakespeare's bland and universal eye
Dwells pleased, through twice a hundred years, on thee.

ALFRED, LORD TENNYSON (1851)

William Charles Macready (1793–1873), contemporary and great
rival of Edmund Kean in London (and of Edwin Forrest in New
York) was also a distinguished theatre manager, who introduced
many reforms in acting and production methods, and helped restore
the true text of Shakespeare's plays.

The Old Playgoer

'Twas after the show, in Public House bar
I met with a man who be-littled our star.
I stood him a drink, and a two D cigar –
                                    He had seen Macready.

I gazed at him wond'ringly – stared at him long –
It rang in my ears like a beautiful song:
The eyes of one man in that commonplace throng
                                    Had beheld – Macready!

'An Actor, a Genius, a Giant! – Sublime!
The "Lane" knew good acting, sir, once on a time;
But now, what is "Hamlet"? Why! mere pantomime!
                                    If you'd seen Macready!'

'The first time I saw him impersonate "Lear"
I sat in the Pit – which cannot be called near,
He precious nigh shattered the drum of my ear –
               He'd a voice – Macready!'

'There isn't an actor in London today.
Don't contradict me, sir! I mean what I say!
Eh? What? No! I never go now to the play!'
               He had seen Macready.

ALBERT CHEVALIER (1903)

To Joe Grimaldi
On his retirement

Joseph! they say thou 'st left the stage,
To toddle down the hill of life,
And taste the flannell'd ease of age,
Apart from pantomimic strife –
Retired (for Young would call it so)
The world shut out – in Pleasant Row!

And hast thou really wash'd at last
From each white cheek the red half-moon
And all thy public Clownship cast,
To play the private Pantaloon!
All youth – all ages yet to be
Shall have a heavy miss of thee!

Thou didst not preach to make us wise –
Thou hadst no finger in our schooling –
Thou didst not 'lure us to the skies' –
Thy simple, simple trade was – Fooling:
And yet, Heav'n knows, we could – we can
Much 'better spare a better man!' . . .

But Joseph – everybody's Joe –
Is gone – and grieve I will and must!
As Hamlet did for Yorick, so
Will I for thee (tho' not yet dust),
And talk as he did when he miss'd
The kissing-crust that he had kiss'd.

Ah, where is now thy rolling head!
Thy winking, reeling, *drunken* eyes,
(As old Catullus would have said)
Thy oven-mouth, that swallow'd pies –
Enormous hunger – monstrous drowth! –
Thy pockets greedy as thy mouth! . . .

Ah, where thy legs – that witty pair!
For 'great wits jump' – and so did they!
Lord! how they leap'd in lamplight air!
Caper'd – and bounced – and strode away:
That years should tame the legs – alack!
I've seen spring through an Almanack! . . .

Oh, how will thy departure cloud
The lamplight of the little breast!
The Christmas child will grieve aloud
To miss his broadest friend and best –
Poor urchin! what avails to him
The cold *New Monthly's* Ghost of Grimm? . . .

Oh, who like thee could ever drink,
Or eat – swill, swallow – bolt – and choke!
Nod, weep and hiccup – sneeze and wink?
Thy very yawn was quite a joke!
Tho' Joseph, junior, acts not ill,
'There's no Fool like the old Fool' still!

Joseph, farewell, dear funny Joe!
We met with mirth – we part in pain!
For many a long long year must go
Ere Fun can see thy like again –
For Nature does not keep great stores
Of perfect Clowns – that are not *Boors*!

THOMAS HOOD (1828)

Joseph Grimaldi (1778–1837), master of every theatrical skill, began his stage life as 'sprite' at Sadler's Wells at the age of two, and thereafter leapt, danced, tumbled, sang, and acted his way to un-challenged supremacy as the Clown of all time. Hood's poem captures some of the delighted affection in which he was held.

'When Crummles Played'

Epilogue to *When Crummles Played*
at the Lyric Theatre, Hammersmith

When Crummles played he never knew
Those pretty arts which charm the few;
He painted with an ampler brush
The coal-black frown, the crimson blush.
No psycho-analytic sage
Had set the farmyard on the stage,
The simple Circles did not itch
To see the bedrooms of the rich;
He kept the awful 'gods' in view
So every devil got his due,
The bigamist was hissed at sight,
And black was black and white was white
    When Crummles played.

It was the player, not the play
That was the thing in Crummles' day;
Maybe it never burned too bright
But still they kept the torch alight:
And we with all our modern arts,
Our subtle, psychic, cocktail-parts,
We who that actor greatest call
Who does not seem to act at all –

Have we, I wonder, earned the right
To laugh at Crummles much tonight?
Though Dickens laughed a little, true,
I think he clapped, so please, won't you,
        'When Crummles played?'

A P HERBERT (1927)

The Crummles family of Dickens' *Nicholas Nickleby* have become the definitive caricature of strolling players of the early nineteenth century. If Dickens had a real Vincent Crummles in mind, it may well have been Thomas Donald Davenport (1792–1851), whose daughter Jean was a true 'Infant Phenomenon'.

John Baldwin Buckstone

Light lie the turf on the old Actor's bier.
    Of many a load he lightened many a heart;
A more mirth-making mimic for many a year
    We are not like to see. 'Tis sad to part,

And leave him lying here out in the cold,
    Who held such cosy corners of our past!
Farewell old 'Bucky', many a heart will hold
    Thy memory green, for all shades o'er it cast!

ANON (1879)

Number One

Star dressing-room –
my prison and my home,
my salvation and my doom,
my Calvary, my Rome.

CYRIL CUSACK (1990)

Mr Beerbohm Tree

He is the very model of the actor (managerial):
He uses Shakespeare's lines to form a sort of ground-
   material.
The bard, in fact, provides the major portion of the letter-
   press:
But the scenery's his own idea. ('Superb! Could not be
   better!' – Press.)

And no maiden at a matinee without a thrill can see
The strange exotic beauty of our only Beerbohm Tree.

   Tree, Tree, Beautiful Tree,
   What a wonderful actor you are!
   You stand all the time,
   In the light of the lime:
   You're a bright and particular star.
   We'd come miles for a sight
   Of that picturesque bend in your knee.
   Our Waller – we love him,
   But rank you above him,
   Our one and our only Tree!

If I'm asked to tell the reasons of his well-earned popularity,
His acting's always funny, while avoiding all vulgarity:
As Hamlet, when he had his conversation with the
   phantom, I'm
Not certain that he didn't beat the leading lights of
   pantomime.
You will burst your waistcoat-buttons, though sewn tightly
   on they be,
If you chance to see the Hamlet of our only Beerbohm
   Tree.

     Tree, Tree, Beautiful Tree.
     May you go from success to success.
     May the crowds block the streets,
     When they're fighting for seats;
     May you never fall out with the Press.
     Though your Antony might
     Be different without vexing me
     Still, the actor who's funny
     Is the man for my money,
     So I'll stick to my Beerbohm Tree.

               P G WODEHOUSE (1907)

Herbert Draper Beerbohm Tree (1852–1917) was actor, manager,
builder of the new Her Majesty's Theatre, founder of the Royal
Academy of Dramatic Art, and, along the way, presenter of lavish
productions. He was knighted in 1909. Lewis Waller (1860–1915)
was the reigning romantic actor of the day – the first of the matinee
idols.

Henry Irving

His life has made this iron age
　More grand and fair in story;
Illumed our Shakespeare's sacred page
　With new and deathless glory;
Refreshed the love of noble fame
　In hearts all sadly faring,
And lit anew the dying flame
　Of genius and of daring.

WILLIAM WINTER (*c* 1885)

Henry Irving (John Henry Brodribb, 1838–1905) was a strange and impressive figure in the line of great English actors, and he dominated the London tragedy stage throughout the late Victorian era. In 1895 he became the first actor to receive a knighthood.

Ellen Terry

In *Charles I* by W G Wills

In the lone tent, waiting for victory,
She stands with eyes marred by the mists of pain,
Like some wan lily overdrenched with rain;
The clamorous clang of arms, the ensanguined sky,
War's ruin, and the wreck of chivalry
To her proud soul no common fear can bring;
Bravely she tarrieth for her Lord, the King,
Her soul aflame with passionate ecstasy.
O, hair of gold! O, crimson lips! O, face
Made for the luring and the love of man!

With thee I do forget the toil and stress,
The loveless road that knows no resting place,
Time's straitened pulse, the soul's dread weariness,
My freedom, and my life republican!

OSCAR WILDE (1879)

The legend of Ellen Terry as Henry Irving's skilled and lovely leading lady at the Lyceum is only part of her story. She was an experienced actress before she met Irving, and a successful manager after she left him. She lived from 1847 to 1928. She was made a Dame of the British Empire in 1925.

The Demon Tragedian

There's some one who lives in the attic
Whose tastes are intensely dramatic;
    'Tis little I'd mind
    But oh! he's inclined
So much to be over-emphatic.

He plays all the leading creations,
Goes in for terrific sensations;
    To hear his Macbeth
    Nearly frightens to death
Myself and my friends and relations.

He says that he means to 'dissemble',
He calls upon tyrants to 'tremble',
    He grunts and he growls,
    And he howls and he scowls,
And think he's Macready or Kemble.

When he struggles to imitate Irving
On me the effect is unnerving,
    I murmur 'Oh! oh!
    Don't torture me so,
Of this I am quite undeserving!'

In tragedy, high and romantic,
His efforts are truly gigantic;
    Of sleep he deprives me,
    And nightly he drives me
As nearly as possible frantic. . . .

He shakes the whole house, and just under
His room it sounds louder than thunder;
    And why the police
    Don't force him to cease,
To me is a matter of wonder.

I've made every effort to stop him,
In pieces I wish I could chop him;
    Or, milder resource, –
    I'd take him by force,
And out of the window I'd drop him!

I'll send a last message, imploring
He'll leave off his ranting and roaring,
    Not stamp overhead
    With elephant tread,
As if he would come through the flooring.

But, bless you! he never would mind me,
Some day 'suicided' you'll find me,
    Unless I take flight
    In the dead of the night,
And leave that tragedian behind me!

WALTER PARKE (1885)

'Untutored Paws'

From *The Prompter*

What could a player of that monster make
Who sets-to acting when he goes to speak!
Then wild in gesture – storming without cause –
He flings at random his untutored paws;
The speech got rid of, mark the mortal then,
What living lumber till he speaks again;
And like a bailiff on a Sunday stands,
Wanting employment for his idle hands.

ANON (1810)

Death of an Actress

I see from the paper that Florrie Forde is dead –
Collapsed after singing to wounded soldiers,
At the age of sixty-five. The American notice
Says no doubt all that need be said

About this one-time chorus girl; whose rôle
For more than forty stifling years was giving
Sexual, sentimental, or comic entertainment,
A gaudy posy for the popular soul.

Plush and cigars: she waddled into the lights,
Old and huge and painted, in velvet and tiara,
Her voice gone but around her head an aura
Of all her vanilla-sweet forgotten vaudeville nights.

With an elephantine shimmy and a sugared wink
She threw a trellis of Dorothy Perkins roses
Around an audience come from slum and suburb
And weary of the tea-leaves in the sink;

Who found her songs a rainbow leading west
To the home they never had, to the chocolate Sunday
Of boy and girl, to cowslip time, to the never-
Ending weekend Islands of the Blest.

In the Isle of Man before the war before
The present one she made a ragtime favourite
Of 'Tipperary', which became the swan-song
Of troop-ships on a darkened shore;

And during Munich sang her ancient quiz
Of *Where's Bill Bailey?* and the chorus answered,
Muddling through and glad to have no answer:
Where's Bill Bailey? How do we know where he is!

Now on a late and bandaged April day
In a military hospital Miss Florrie
Forde has made her positively last appearance
And taken her bow and correctly gone away.

Correctly. For she stood
For an older England, for children toddling
Hand in hand while the day was warm and bright.
    Let the wren and robin
Gently with leaves cover the Babes in the Wood.

LOUIS MACNEICE (1940)

Chaplin

The sun, a heavy spider, spins in the thirsty sky.
The wind hides under cactus leaves, in doorway corners.
  Only the wry

Small shadow accompanies Hamlet-Petrouchka's march –
  the slight
Wry sniggering shadow in front in the morning turning at
  noon, behind towards night.

The plumed cavalcade has passed to to-morrow, is lost
    again;
But the wisecrack-mask, the quick-flick-fanfare of the cane
    remain.

Diminuendo of footsteps even is done:
Only remain, Don Quixote, hat, cane, smile and sun.

Goliaths fall to our sling, but craftier fates than these
Lie ambushed – malice of open manholes, strings in the
    dark and falling trees.

God kicks our backsides, scatters peel on the smoothest
    stair;
And towering centaurs steal the tulip lips, the aureoled hair,

While we, craned from the gallery, throw our cardboard
    flowers
And our feet jerk to tunes not played for ours.

                              A S J TESSIMOND (1934)

Rudolph Valentino Comes to Heaven

He was so slight a thing,
he was so white a thing,
with his beautiful body, and the sinuous grace
        of his tenuous face.

He was so young a thing,
he was so unwrung a thing
with his easy movement, and the limber charm
        with slumber warm.

He was so unbroken a thing,
so half-woken a thing,
with his ignorant beauty, and air of a stupid
        theatrical cupid.

He was so adored a thing,
he was so bored a thing,
with no knowledge, no wisdom, and the loneliness
　　of his wistful unmanliness.

He was so unintentional a thing,
he was so one-dimensional a thing,
that he smiled at the gate, as though heavenly peace
　　were a film to release.

He was so untaught a thing,
he was so death-caught a thing,
that he smiled at the gate, as though Peter were
　　his own photographer.

He was so trifling a thing,
he was so heart-rifling a thing,
that an angel was caught by the nebulous grace
　　of his fabulous face,

and seeing him so mean a thing,
so in-between a thing,
cried to St Peter: 'O Peter, be merciful
　　to this mock-Parsifal.

'Since he's so frail a thing,
so a boy's-tale a thing
of youth's arrogant splendour, let us restore to him
　　what life was before to him.

'Let him for ever be
only a mimicry,
only a shadow, a hint and a guess
　　at loveliness.

'Silver in mail and helm
in an eternal film,
let him go flashing, as if he played
　　in a crusade.

'Make a new thing of him,
an untrue Spring of him,
and a shadow shall be heaven by shadows enticed for
  .him,
and a shadow be God, and a shadow be Christ for him.'

HUMBERT WOLFE (1927)

Laurence Olivier's Richard III

Yes, we have journeyed up from the iron vessel
Lying like a queen in the drenched Scottish landscape,
The sullen Clyde oozing into the Turner sunset.
We have booked a bed at the Greenock YMCA, and fled
To Glasgow and the last-minute six-and-sixpenny upper-
  box.
The excited programme, no time for a wet in the bar,
The Sickert plush and the white arm adoring the 'cello,
Sweet excitement of strings, and up like a trumpet note flies
  the easy curtain
And Richard of England comes limping into the thick air
Of velvet and drums, crown and ermine and scarlet,
And the wanton flags licking like tongues the brilliant blue
  bowl of the morning.

HMS Glory   CHARLES CAUSLEY (1945)

To Peggy Ashcroft

There is a beauty we should not assess –
– The unconscious accident of perfect form:
We analyse – to find it has grown less,
And first amazement withers into scorn.
Your beauty is no accident. It lives
In each well-judged expression of your art,
And the enchantment of the whole survives
Analysis of each specific part.

ACTORS

Your tenderest simplicity can teem
With intricate complexities of skill,
And yet the skill can make the complex seem
A natural impulse – not an act of will;
While fantasy more rich than any dream
Lacquers this magic with more magic still.

STEPHEN HAGGARD (1939)

The Actor

Here's my cue
delivered deliberately.
Did *I* say that?
Now – it's you.

A listening lot of
upturned faces
are waiting for
– who knows what?

These are not my words I'm saying.
This dress belongs to another age.
Moving to order to sit on a chair,
to show an emotion that I don't share.
Responding, reacting as if I care.
Perhaps after all the world *is* a stage!

My lines I've rendered
gesticulating defiantly,
Delivering the message
as the author intended.

All can see
it's interpretive puppetry.
So, whatever happened
to me?

KATIE PARKER (1982)

Alpha Beta

Actor and actress
After three acts of hatred
Meet the audience
Face to face – free of the scenes:
They hold hands, they kiss, and bow.

TOM DURHAM (1973)

Last Night

And so they parted as the curtain fell,
Who'd worked together for a dream or more.
Another batch of back-stage yarns to tell –
Another wolf kept, briefly, from the door.
These lines again may never more be spoke:
These songs again may never more be sung.
Now silent once again are chord and tongue,
Dispersed the funny, secret, theatre folk . . .

NICHOLAS SMITH (1968)

On Actors

They cry, when critics cook their goose:
'That isn't criticism – it's just abuse!'
But where's the actor who, belauded, says:
'That isn't criticism – it's merely praise!'?

HERBERT FARJEON (1942)

Ballade of Dead Actors

Where are the passions they essayed,
And where the tears they made to flow?
Where the wild humours they portrayed
For laughing worlds to see and know?
Othello's wrath and Juliet's woe?
Sir Peter's whims and Timon's gall?
And Millamant and Romeo?
Into the night go one and all.

Where are the braveries, fresh or frayed?
The plumes, the armours – friend and foe?
The cloth of gold, the rare brocade,
The mantles glittering to and fro?
The pomp, the pride, the royal show?
The cries of war and festival?
The youth, the grace, the charm, the glow?
Into the night go one and all.

The curtain falls, the play is played:
The Beggar packs beside the Beau;
The Monarch troops, and troops the Maid;
The Thunder huddles with the Snow.
Where are the revellers high and low?
The clashing swords? The lover's call?
The dancers gleaming row on row?
Into the night go one and all.

Envoy:

Prince, in one common overthrow
The Hero tumbles with the Thrall:
As dust that drives, as straws that blow,
Into the night go one and all.

W E HENLEY (*c* 1898)

'Walking Shadows'

The poet to the end of time,
Breathes in his works and lives in rhyme;
But when the actor sinks to rest,
And the turf lies upon his breast,
A poor traditionary fame
Is all that's left to grace his name.

WILLIAM COMBE (1809)

PARTS

Our Garrick's a salad; for in him we see
Oil, vinegar, sugar, and saltness agree.

OLIVER GOLDSMITH (1774)

The Repertory Actor

The repertory actor earns
    My very high respect,
For think of all the parts he learns
    And has to recollect;
And when he acts in Shakespeare's plays
    His life's an almost hopeless maze.

On Monday, as *Antonio*,
    He dodges *Shylock's* knife;
On Tuesday, being *Prospero*,
    He leads the simple life;
On Thursday he must go to death
    As *Lear*; on Friday as *Macbeth*.

At Wednesday's matinée he's made
    To play the fool and chaff
As *Touchstone*, or as *Quince* he's paid
    To make the children laugh;
At night he must appear again
    To play the melancholy Dane.

*   *   *

Oh, why is *Juliet* amazed?
    Why does she turn her back
On *Romeo*, and look so dazed?
    By Jove, his face is black!
He thinks it is the night, poor fellow,
    On which he has to play *Othello*.

GUY BOAS (1925)

'The Natural'

Momus would act the fool's part in a play,
And 'cause he would be exquisite that way,
Hies me to London, where no day can pass,
But that some play-house still his presence has.
Now at the Globe with a judicious eye,
Into the vice's action doth he pry.
Next to the Fortune, where it is a chance
But he marks something worth his cognisance.
Then to the Curtain, where, as at the rest,
He notes that action down that likes him best.
Being full fraught, at length he gets him home,
And Momus, now, knows how to play the Mome . . .
Fie on this mimic still, it mars his part:
Nature would do far better without art.

JOHN HEATH (1610)

An Elegy on our Late Protean Roscius Richard Burbage

No more young Hamlet though but scant of breath
Shall cry revenge for his dear father's death:
Poor Romeo never more shall tears beget
For Juliet's love and cruel Capulet;
Harry shall not be seen as King or Prince,
They died with thee, Dear Dick –
Not to revive again. Jeronimo
Shall cease to mourn his son Horatio;
They cannot call thee from thy naked bed
By horrid outcry; and Antonio's dead.
Edward shall lack a representative,
And Crookback, as befits, shall cease to live.
Tyrant Macbeth, with unwash'd bloody hand
We vainly now may hope to understand.

Brutus and Marcius henceforth must be dumb,
For ne'er thy like upon our stage shall come
To charm the faculty of eyes and ears,
Unless we could command the dead to rise.
Vindex is gone, and what a loss was he!
Frankford, Brachiano and Malevole
Heart-broke Philaster and Amintas too
Are lost for ever; with the red-haired Jew,
Which sought the brankrupt merchant's pound of flesh,
By woman-lawyer caught in his own mesh.
What a wide world was in that little space,
Thyself a world, the Globe thy fittest place!
Thy stature small, but every thought and mood
Might thoroughly from thy face be understood,
And his whole action he could change with ease
From ancient Lear to youthful Pericles.
But let me not forget one chiefest part,
Wherein beyond the rest, he moved the heart,
The grieved Moor, made jealous by a slave
Who sent his wife to fill a timeless grave,
Then slew himself upon the bloody bed.
All these and many more with him are dead,
Thereafter must our poets leave to write.
Since thou art gone, dear Dick, a tragic night
Will wrap our black-hung stage. He made a Poet,
And those who yet remain full surely know it;
For having Burbage to give forth each line
It filled their brain with fury more divine.

ANON (1619)

'Macklin's Shylock'

This is the Jew
That Shakespeare drew.

ALEXANDER POPE
(1741)

Two Lears

The town has found out different ways,
    To praise its different Lears;
To Barry it gives loud huzzas,
    To Garrick only tears.

A king? Ay, every inch a king –
    Such Barry doth appear;
But Garrick's quite another thing;
    He's every inch *King Lear*.

RICHARD KENDAL (1811)

The Latest Hamlet

An Acrostic

I

H ow various, in the Stage's restless reign,
A re these successive portraits of the Dane!
M ajestic or familiar, bold or mild,
L oving or harsh, loud, quiet, tame or wild,
E ach type in turn the drama has supplied,
T ill only Shakespeare could their claims decide.

II

W hat is this last? A fresh impetuous youth
I ntense in scorn of guile and love of truth,
L ost in a moral maze, without a clue,
S uspecting all, or trusting very few;
O ft wavering in revenge's deadly plan;
N o demigod or hero, but a man.

III

B ut is this Shakespeare's Hamlet? who can tell?
A ll that we know is this – it pleases well,
R ightly or wrongly, such a Prince as he
R eflects our nature, wins our sympathy,
E merges safe from criticism's storm,
T o face the crowds who greet, with welcome warm,
'T he glass of fashion and the mould of form.'

WALTER PARKE (1885)

Wilson Barrett (1847–1904) is remembered more for melodrama than for Shakespeare. His fortune was made not by leaping into Ophelia's grave in *Hamlet* but by being thrown to the lions in *The Sign of the Cross*.

Robert Lindsay's Hamlet
(for Braham Murray)

That's him, in the foetal position, among
The front row watchers,

Sweatshirt and jeans, nothing particular, you
Wouldn't look twice, till

He stands to pace that eccentric circuit, from
Clouds still hang on you

To *Cracks a noble heart*, with the special props
That signal the Prince:

Two swords, recorders, skulls, a cup and a book.
The junk has banked up

Along the years. He can't move a foot without
Dislodging clinker –

First Folio, the good Quarto, bright guesses
From dead editors,

A notion of Goethe's, a sad hometruth of
Seedy STC's,

Business inherited from great-grandfathers
Garrick, Kean, Irving –

Heir to all this, as his watchers are heirs
Of dead playgoers,

Coming to see what they already know, with
Astonish me! smiles.

Who could mine anything new from this heap of
Old British rubbish?

But this man, discarding limelight and ketchup,
Customary suits,

Delivered raw at each performance, elbows
Us along the trite

Life of the man who thought faster than anyone ever, till we,

Losing our poise, are lost, like the ignorant
Playgoer, watching

The story, whispering at the wrong moment
Does he kill him now?

U A FANTHORPE (1984)

Essentials to Shakespeare

I am the man who enters once. I am
The serving maid who never speaks. I am
The boy who carries a stool,
The woman who cooks a meal,
A mother who quiets her child.
I stand in the wings and I
Prompt. I am part of the stage sets, I
Help with the lights and I
Am essential to a great
Tragedy. I help
The jokes on in happier plays.
You do not see me. I don't appeal to the senses.
I am Shakespeare's intention. He let me loose
Between his lines. Nobody claps or cheers.
Perhaps I seem dumb or blind.
But without me none of these plays could ever go on.
I am lodged in Shakespeare's mind.

ELIZABETH JENNINGS (1985)

An Actor

A shabby fellow chanced one day to meet
The British Roscius in the street,
    Garrick, of whom our nation justly brags;
The fellow hugged him with a kind embrace; –
'Good sir, I do not recollect your face,'
    Quoth Garrick. 'No?' replied the man of rags;
'The boards of Drury you and I have trod
    Full many a time together, I am sure.'

'When?' with an oath, cried Garrick, 'for, by G–d,
I never saw that face of yours before!
     What characters, I pray,
      Did you and I together play?'
'Lord!' quoth the fellow, 'think not that I mock –
When you played Hamlet, sir, I played the cock!'

PETER PINDAR (JOHN WOLCOT) (1786)

The Super

    A super!
    A shilling mute –
  A soldier in a cast-off suit,
    A robber bold,
    A peasant old,
     A sprite.
I don't stick out for terms: a bob a night.

    A super!
    Ambitious? No.
 I find out as I older grow
    Those built that way
    Ain't built to stay;
     It kills.
You'll never see my name, sir, in the bills.

    A super!
    To cheer and shout –
  A ruffian for the Star to clout,
    A belted earl,
    A low-born churl.
    No height
I cannot scale – or fall from – bob a night!

A super!
And yet I've lent
A trifle to a leading gent,
With wife and kids.
He'd signed for 'quids' –
A sign
His screw was not a certainty – like mine.

A super!
A Capulet
(In 'Romeo and Juliet')
At a given cue,
A Montagu
To fight.
A thief, a saint – same price, sir: bob a night!

ALBERT CHEVALIER (1903)

The Extra

Indeed, I saw Romeo
That day, shortly before
The killings. He wore
Purple breeches, I know
Because I marked it to my sister.

He was young and flush
Under a hot sun's unclouded sky.
He smiled at me as he went by
To the big square where the fountains rush
In arcs at each other's throats.

Shall I say what happened then?
There were voices abrading the still of the heat;
I squinted at shutters across a side-street,
Dust spumed gracefully and two men,
Arm round waist, limped toward shadow.

It's hard to say what happened next.
I thought Tybalt had fled
But there he was again – dead
In a minute! This was some test
Of nerve, I suppose, and honour.

It was bad, really, the way they used this town,
You couldn't buy a button or wash a sock
Without thinking you'd be better under lock
And key while Verona was their battleground.
I wouldn't want my kids to grow up with that.

All the same, he was a nice boy,
That Romeo. His future looked good as well.
I mean, his family was right, you could tell
At a glance he was going one way –
Up – but now he's just a might-have-been.

Of course, I can't complain about the tourist trade.
Star-crossed buns and badges 're always in demand,
We sell Juliet ribbons by royal command . . .
Ah, Juliet! A very pretty girl, made
In heaven, you might say, and barely unwrapped.

Well, I'd best get back to the grind.
I hope you've got your story –
Plenty of tears and not much glory!
Look at the tomb if you've a mind,
You have to pay – ah, thanks! – but it's worth the time.

ALAN DUNNETT (1984)

In Pursuit of a Bear

The rôle of Antigonus in THE WINTER'S TALE
Was created by one Mackeson, of Evesham Vale;
And this Other William had the honour to share
In a stage-direction beyond compare,
'Exit, pursued by a bear.'

Who created the part of the pursuant brute?
A real ursine actor? Two men in a bear-suit?
Ursa Major, Minor? Orson? What was his name,
This grizzly mummer of Globe Theatre fame?
Teddy, Pooh, Paddington much later came.

Travelling with ULYSSES, the siren voice
Comes in stream-of-self-consciousness from James Joyce!
(My pursuit of him necessary, not by choice)
Eureka! The bear who corpsed poor Will Mackeson
Was an upstaging pit-growler called Sackerson.

MARIE ANTHONY (1970)

Sackerson was a celebrated old bear kept in the Thames-side Bear
Garden. Shakespeare mentions him in *The Merry Wives of Windsor*,
when he makes Slender boast to Anne Page: 'I have seen Sackerson
loose twenty times, and have taken him by the chain.'

Act V, Scene 5

You call the old nurse and the little page
To act survivors on your tragic stage –
You love the intrusive extra character.
'But where's the tragedy,' you say, 'should none
Remain to moralize on what's been done?
Such silence trembles with a sort of laughter.
Tears purge the soul: the nurse's broken line
"O mistress, pretty one, dead!" the page's whine
"Thou too? Alas, fond master!"'

No purge for my disgusted soul, no tears
Will wash away my bile of tragic years,
No sighs vicariously abate my rancour –
If nurse and page survive, I'd have them own
Small sorrow to be left up-stage alone,
And on the bloodiest field of massacre
Either rant out the anti-climax thus:
'A's dead, the bitch!' 'So's Oscar! Joy for us!'
Then fall to rifling pocket, belt and purse
With corky jokes and pantomime of sin;
Or let the feud rage on, page against nurse –
His jewelled dirk, her thundrous rolling-pin.

ROBERT GRAVES (1930)

The Changeling, to Oberon

Sir, I await you on the shore, alone,
  Standing in a cold rivulet, the dark water
    Racing past my ankles.

I hear the shuffle of waves, and see the moonrise.
  Then I shall see the tails of your magnificent dolphins
    Bearing you inshore, and I will run
      Into the right arm of your greeting,
        As all the sunken bells peal in the depths of the
          water.

I have obtained evergreens and plaited them into a crown.
  I will lead you through the white satin of a waterfall
    To my round cave, piled high with golden bracken.
      I have caught two black lobsters, and taught them
        dancing.

There is mead of my brewing, and small white cakes
  Baked on hot stones. I promise you my hedgehog and
    my mouse.
    Sir, secure me from the spells of Puck.
      Appoint me a place in your dark empire.

JONATHAN FIELD (1966)

Instructions to an Actor

Now, boy, remember this is the great scene.
You'll stand on a pedestal behind a curtain,
the curtain will be drawn, and you don't move
for eighty lines; don't move, don't speak, don't breathe.
I'll stun them all out there, I'll scare them,
make them weep, but it depends on you.
I warn you eighty lines is a long time,
but you don't breathe, you're dead,
you're a dead queen, a statue,
you're dead as stone, new-carved,
new-painted and the paint not dry
– we'll get some red to keep your lip shining –

and you're a mature woman, you've got dignity,
some beauty still in middle-age, and
you're kind and true, but you're dead,
your husband thinks you're dead,
the audience thinks you're dead,
and you don't breathe, boy, I say
you don't even blink for eighty lines,
if you blink you're out!
Fix your eye on something and keep watching it.
Practise when you get home. It can be done.
And you move at last – music's the cue.
When you hear a mysterious solemn jangle
of instruments, make yourself ready.
Five lines more, you can lift a hand.
It may tingle a bit, but lift it –
slow, slow –
O this is where I hit them
right between the eyes, I've got them now –
I'm making the dead walk –
you move a foot, slow, steady, down,
you guard your balance in case you're stiff,
you move, you step down, down from the pedestal,
control your skirt with one hand, the other hand
you now hold out –
O this will melt their hearts if nothing does –
to your husband who wronged you long ago
and hesitates in amazement
to believe you are alive.
Finally he embraces you, and there's nothing
I can give you to say, boy,
but you must show that you have forgiven him.
Forgiveness, that's the thing. It's like a second life.
I know you can do it. – Right then, shall we try?

EDWIN MORGAN (1977)

The poet imagines Shakespeare directing the boy-actor who first
played the part of Hermione in *A Winter's Tale*.

Mime

on the black stage he
was in an imaginary box
mime mime mime mime mi

its inner surface stopped his
hand. the audience gasped
amazing amazing amazing ama

he climbed stairs that were
not there, walked and went
nowhere nowhere nowhere now

the real world was what his
head told his hands to delimit
in air in air in air in a

chill certain as glass. the
other world was fuzzy and
treacherous treacherous trea

he took a plane, it began
to fall, the passengers shrieked
help o God o help help he

the mime imagined a box.
his feet hit glass, the plane's
fall halted. up, up. praise be
mimesis mimesis mimesis mime

JOHN UPDIKE (*c* 1968)

Shakespeare's Hotspur

He gurgled beautifully on television,
playing your death, that Shakespearian actor.
Blood glugged under his tongue, he gagged on
words, as you did, Hotspur, Hotspur:
it was an arrow killed you, not a prince,
not Hal clashing over you in his armour,
stabbing featly for the cameras, and your face
unmaimed. You fell into the hands of Shakespeare,
were given a lovely fluency,
undone, redone, made his creature.
In life you never found it easy
to volley phrases off into the future.
And as for your death scene, that hot day
at Shrewsbury you lifted your visor:
a random arrow smashed into your eye
and mummed your tongue-tied mouth for ever.

FLEUR ADCOCK (1983)

In Bed with Macbeth

I hear him now, the candle gutters
On his wrist. I can't close my eyes,
The bone-rings clench my jaw, it stutters
Inside the skull, cold water in drips.

He puts his back to me and sighs
Like a mouse lamed in a trap –
Every night the same but neither cries,
Staring and apart in one big coffin.

I take my hand and make it slip
Between his legs, to stop the thinking.
He twists his neck and bites my lips,
Our gooseflesh chafes the bed-fur.

He drags my head down to his lap
And knots my hair in his fist.
A child calls twice and the moon wraps
Herself in a mist for shame.

If I held a cup now, I'd let it sip
Until I were drowned in the drinking.
I'd take my hands and make them dip
In the wine to make the nails clean.

If I held a knife now, I'd let it drive
Between my eye and my crack.
If I were a child and called out twice,
Would my mother come for my sin?

I hear him now, he groans and mutters,
And swears by his Christ as he lies.
And now he starts his dead man's shudders,
Whilst I brood my sores to the quick.

ALAN DUNNETT (1983)

Fleance

I entered with a torch before me
And cast my shadow on the backcloth
Momentarily: a handful of words,
One bullet with my initials on it –
And that got stuck in a property tree.

I would have caught it between my teeth
Or, a true professional, stood still
While the two poetic murderers
Pinned my silhouette to history
In a shower of accurate daggers.

But as any illusionist might
Unfasten the big sack of darkness,
The ropes and handcuffs, and emerge
Smoking a nonchalant cigarette,
I escaped – only to lose myself.

It took me a lifetime to explore
The dusty warren beneath the stage
With its trapdoor opening on to
All that had happened above my head
Like noises–off or distant weather.

In the empty auditorium I bowed
To one preoccupied caretaker
And, without removing my make-up,
Hurried back to the digs where Banquo
Sat up late with a hole in his head.

MICHAEL LONGLEY (c 1973)

The Actor

His mind soars on thespian wings
O'er rent, rates, taxes – sordid things;
His voice breathes magic even when
He merely says, 'It's half-past ten.'

Strindbergers do his palate please,
His oaths are strange Ibsenities;
If outrageous fortune slings too hard
He quotes at Will from the Immortal Bard.

When Misanthropic, I declare
He's down to playing Molière;
One angry look at me, his wife,
Is Jimmy Porter to the life.

Yet, Romeo-antic when alone,
With just a soupçon of Touchstone;
He holds me warmly in his heart,
Right next to his Dramatic Art.

He really lives his rôles, you see,
And that is why I sigh, 'Ah me!
Will this run be ever-lasting?
Don Juan is such Hellish casting.'

MARIE ANTHONY (1973)

Private Theatricals
Lady Arabella Fustian to Lord Clarence Fustian

> Sweet when Actors first appear,
> The loud collision of applauding gloves!
> Moultrie

Your labours, my talented brother,
    Are happily over at last;
They tell me that, somehow or other,
    The Bill is rejected – or past:
And now you'll be coming, I'm certain,
    As fast as four posters can crawl,
To help us to draw up our curtain,
    As usual, at Fustian Hall.

Arrangements are nearly completed;
    But still we've a lover or two,
Whom Lady Albina entreated
    We'd keep, at all hazards, for you:
Sir Arthur makes horrible faces –
    Lord John is a trifle too tall –
And yours are the safest embraces
    To faint in, at Fustian Hall. . . .

Bye the bye, there are two or three matters
    We want you to bring us from Town;
The Inca's white plumes from the hatter's,
    A nose and a hump for the clown:
We want a few harps at our banquet;
    We want a few masques for our ball;
And steal from your wise friend Bosanquet
    His white wig, for Fustian Hall. . . .

And, Clarence, you'll really delight us,
    If you'll do your endeavour to bring
From the Club a young person to write us
    Our prologue, and that sort of thing;
Poor Crotchet, who did them supremely
    Is gone, for a Judge, to Bengal;
I fear we shall miss him extremely
    This season, at Fustian Hall.

Come, Clarence – your idol Albina
    Will make a sensation, I feel;
We all think there never was seen a
    Performer so like the O'Neill:
At rehearsals, her exquisite fury
    Has deeply affected us all;
For one tear that trickles at Drury,
    There'll be twenty at Fustian Hall. . . .

She stabbed a bright mirror this morning –
    Poor Kitty was quite out of breath –
And trampled in anger and scorning,
    A bonnet and feathers to death.
But hark – I've a part in 'The Stranger' –
    There's the Prompter's detestable call:
Come, Clarence – our Romeo and Ranger,
    We want you at Fustian Hall.

W M PRAED (*c* 1830)

The Villains at the 'Vic'

A Song

All the world's a stage, the men and women merely players,
  Buskin strollers on the look out for a pitch,
A motley group of decent people, fools and their betrayers,
  And it's hard to tell exactly which is which.
Acting is a lost art. I was young and once aspiring,
  All my friends informed me I should do the trick;
Now I'm going to give it up; I was not so retiring
  When I used to play the Villains at the Vic.

When I used to play the Villains at the Vic.,
At crime I never yet was known to stick,
  I murdered babes by dozens,
    Slew innumerable cousins,
When I used to play the Villains at the Vic.

What is acting now-a-days? Why only milk-and-water;
  Do you ever see six murders in a play?
An unforgiving parent plunge a dagger in his daughter?
  Yet they did it in a happy bygone day.
Realism, bah! It's only cuff and collar shooting,
  Pooh! Such figures into shape you cannot lick;
You should have heard the gods vociferously hooting,
  When I used to play the Villains at the Vic.

When I used to play, &c.

Look at modern playbills! Well, to me they're simply
    funny,
  How on earth they ever get the people in!
Eight o'clock to start, and only one piece for your money,
  Ah! Much earlier at the Vic did we begin.

Farce at seven, quickly followed by *Maria Martin*,
   And although against the business I might kick,
Change I had to for the panto, which I had a part in,
   When I used to play the Villains at the Vic.

When I used to play, &c.

ALBERT CHEVALIER (1894)

Gus: The Theatre Cat

Gus is the Cat at the Theatre Door.
His name, as I ought to have told you before,
Is really Asparagus. That's such a fuss
To pronounce, that we usually call him just Gus.
His coat's very shabby, he's thin as a rake,
And he suffers from palsy that makes his paw shake.
Yet he was, in his youth, quite the smartest of Cats –
But no longer a terror to mice and to rats.

For he isn't the Cat that he was in his prime;
Though his name was quite famous, he says, in its time.
And whenever he joins his friends at their club
(Which takes place at the back of the neighbouring pub)
He loves to regale them, if someone else pays,
With anecdotes drawn from his palmiest days.
For he once was a Star of the highest degree –
He has acted with Irving, he's acted with Tree.
And he likes to relate his success on the Halls,
Where the Gallery once gave him seven cat-calls.
But his grandest creation, as he loves to tell,
Was Firefrorefiddle, the Fiend of the Fell.

'I have played,' so he says, 'every possible part,
And I used to know seventy speeches by heart.
I'd extemporize back-chat, I knew how to gag,
And I knew how to let the cat out of the bag.

PARTS

I knew how to act with my back and my tail;
With an hour of rehearsal, I never could fail.
I'd a voice that would soften the hardest of hearts,
Whether I took the lead, or in character parts.
I have sat by the bedside of poor Little Nell;
When the Curfew was rung, then I swung on the bell.
In the Pantomime season I never fell flat,
And I once understudied Dick Whittington's Cat.
But my grandest creation, as history will tell,
Was Firefrorefiddle, the Fiend of the Fell.'

Then, if someone will give him a toothful of gin,
He will tell how he once played a part in *East Lynne*.
At a Shakespeare performance he once walked on pat,
When some actor suggested the need for a cat.
He once played a Tiger – could do it again –
Which an Indian Colonel pursued down a drain.
And he thinks that he still can, much better than most,
Produce blood-curdling noises to bring on the Ghost.
And he once crossed the stage on a telegraph wire,
To rescue a child when a house was on fire.
And he says: 'Now, these kittens, they do not get trained
As we did in the days when Victoria reigned.
They never get drilled in a regular troupe,
And they think they are smart, just to jump through a
  hoop.'

And he'll say, as he scratches himself with his claws,
'Well, the Theatre's certainly not what it was.
These modern productions are all very well,
But there's nothing to equal, from what I hear tell,
    That moment of mystery
    When I made history
As Firefrorefiddle, the Fiend of the Fell.'

T S ELIOT (1939)

The Night I Appeared as Macbeth

A Song

'Twas at a YMCA concert
I craved a desire for the stage.
In Flanders one night I was asked to recite,
Gadzooks, I was quickly the rage.
They said I was better than Irving,
And gave me some biscuits and tea.
I know it's not union wages,
But that was the usual fee.
Home I came, bought a dress,
Appeared in your Theatre and what a success!

    I acted so tragic the house rose like magic,
    The audience yelled 'You're sublime!'
    They made me a present of Mornington Crescent,
    They threw it a brick at a time.
    Someone threw a fender which caught me a bender,
    I hoisted a white flag and tried to surrender.
    They jeered me, they queered me,
    And half of them stoned me to death.
    They threw nuts and sultanas, fried eggs and bananas,
    The night I appeared as Macbeth.

The play tho' ascribed to Bill Shakespeare,
To me lacked both polish and tone,
So I put bits in from Miss Elinor Glyn,
Nat Gould and some bits of my own.
The band played *The Barber of Seville*
And being too long they made cuts,
Then I entered somewhere in Scotland
And finished in Newington Butts.
Oh, the flowers, what a feast!
They threw it in bagfuls, self-raising and yeast.

I acted so tragic the house rose like magic,
I improved the part with a dance.
The pit had a relapse, so RAMC chaps
Were wired for to come back from France.
I withdrew my sabre, and started to labour,
Cried 'Lay on Macduff' to my swash-buckling
   neighbour,
I hollared 'I'm collared,
I must reach the bridge or it's death!'
But they altered my journey, I reached the infirmary,
The night I appeared as Macbeth.

The advertised time for the curtain
Was six forty-five on the sheet;
The hall-keeper he having mislaid the key
We played the first act in the street.
Then some-body called for the author,
'He's dead' said the flute player's wife.
The news caused an awful commotion
And gave me the shock of my life.
Shakespeare dead? Poor old Bill!
Why I never knew the poor fellow was ill.

I acted so tragic the house rose like magic,
They wished David Garrick could see,
But he's in the Abbey, then someone quite shabby
Suggested that's where I should be.
Lloyd George and Clemenceau they both carried on so
The King of the Belgians rushed in with Alfonso.
They pleaded unheeded
And all of them cried in one breath
'There's another war coming if you don't stop
   humming,'
The night I appeared as Macbeth.

I acted so tragic the house rose like magic,
I gave them such wonderful thrills,
My tender emotion caused so much commotion
The dress circle made out their wills;
The gallery boys straining dropped tears uncomplaining,
The pit put umbrellas up, thought it was raining.
Some floated, some boated,
And five of the band met their death,
And the poor programme women sold programmes
    while swimming,
The night I appeared as Macbeth.

WILLIAM HARGREAVES (1922)

BACKSTAGE

Say, who conducts that grand, superb machine,
 By which three Muses, loveliest of the Nine,
  With pen and pencil, and with voice, combine
To charm, delight – himself the while unseen.

JOHN O'KEEFFE (1826)

Song of the Stage-Hands

We work in the wings
At various things
That nobody sees from the stalls:
You don't think of us
Unless there's a fuss
And bits of the scenery falls.
But what would be seen of the old Fairy Queen
If the Palace came down on her head?
The actors may bark: but if they're in the dark
It don't matter what Shakespeare said.
It's the same thing wherever you go:
The bloke in the front gets the show.
    But where would he be
    If it wasn't for we –
Working away in the wings?

It looks all serene:
You see a new scene –
From the bed–chamber, say, to the Yacht.
    But you'd change your mind
    If you came round behind
And saw what a job we have got.
We lower the mast but the damn thing sticks fast:
    The rigging is foul of the punt.
We push houses round, but we mayn't make a sound,
    For the hero's proposing in front.
And then, when we change to the wood,
With the moon coming out as it should,
    Well, give us a hand,
    The invisible band,
Working away in the wings.

But still we're all proud
We're one of the crowd
That's pulling the jolly old strings:
 For, bless you, we know
 We're as much in the show
As the fellow who dances or sings.
We've got no bouquets, and they don't wait for days
 To see us come out of the door.
We can't write a play, but if we go away
There won't be no plays any more.

But there – though we bark we don't bite:
It'll all be right on the night.
 Enjoy yourselves, do:
 For we'll see you through,
Working away in the wings.

A P HERBERT (1948)

Sammy Slap the Bill Sticker

From a Street Ballad

Round Nelson's statty, Charing Cross, vhen anything's the
 go, Sirs,
You'll always find me at my post, a sticking up the Posters,
I've hung Macready twelve feet high, – and though it may
 seem funny,
Day after day against the valls, I've plastered Mrs Honey!

Now often, in the vay of trade, and I don't care a farden,
Arter I have been vell paid to hang for Common Garden,
Old Drury Lane has called me in, with jealousy to cover
 'em,
And sent me round vith their own bills, to go and plaster
 over 'em.

I'm proud to say there's Helen Tree, the stage's great
  adorner,
I've had the honour of posting her in every hole and corner,
And Helen Faucit – bless her eyes! ve use her pretty freely,
And paste's Madame Vestris bang atop of Mr Keeley!

Sometimes I'm jobbing for the Church, vith Charitable
  Sermons,
And sometimes for theatres, vith the English and the
  Germans;
To me, in course, no odds it is, as long as I'm a vinner,
Vhether I works for a Saint, or hangs up for a Sinner.

ANON (1800s)

Wilde

Prompter to Covent Garden Theatre

Say, who conducts that grand superb machine,
  By which three Muses, loveliest of the Nine,
  With pen and pencil, and with voice, combine
To charm, delight – himself the while unseen:
  Not like Italian Opera prompting chap,
  Who thrusts his pate and snuff-box up the trap;
Our English prompter keeps beside the scene.

The play received, by manager 'tis cast:
  Aloud in green-room to performers read,
  Each keeps his eye upon his part – nought said.
Rehearsal's call'd, and, from the first to last,
  The prompter on the stage at table sits:
  He vers'd in works of great and little wits,
What safe and dangerous can with art contrast.

Thro' dressing-rooms is heard the warning call,
  'First music, gentlemen; first music, ladies:'
'Third music!' that's the notice to appal;
  Like summons from Lord Mayor, or huffing cadies:
The call-boy is this herald's appellation.
The curtain up, the prompter takes his station.

'Tis not alone with art to throw the word,
  If actors in their parts should make a stand;
To prompter many duties more belong,
  Than binding at the wing with book in hand.
Of their go-off, come-on, he points the sides,
  By margin letters of PS OP
Stage properties, stage business, music, band,
  Of stage arcana prompter keeps the key.
He writes the playbills out, pens paragraphs,
  Marks forfeits down for every stage neglect.
The audience gone, he, ere the lights are out,
  Of all new scenes tries every new effect:
And, from eleven o'clock, perhaps till three,
  He in his duty all that time must spend;
And then from six to twelve o'clock at night,
  Upon the stage the Prompter must attend.

Though folks who come and pay to be amused,
  Have with such petty trifles no concern.
The wisest of us all more wise may be,
  And all must be more wise the more they learn.

This Prompter Wilde, no stir, no bustle made,
  By gentle means did all he had to do;
With diligence his task he well perform'd,
  And prompted of my plays just forty-two.

As thro' the churchyard, walking with his friend,
  That friend was Palmer, Liverpool the town,
Each chose his grave, and awful was the choice,
  Fate gave the word, Death rang the curtain down.

JOHN O'KEEFFE (1826)

'Tragic Trappings'

Hung be the heavens with black, yield day to night!

WILLIAM SHAKESPEARE (*c* 1590)

The stage is hung with black; and I perceive
The auditors prepared for tragedy.

ANON (*c* 1590)

Black stage for tragedies and murder fell!

WILLIAM SHAKESPEARE (*c* 1593)

If this green cloth could speak, could it not tell,
Upon its well-worn nap how oft I fell?
To death in various forms delivered up
Steel kills me one night, and the next the cup.

DAVID GARRICK (1777)

Omnipotent Design

From *Expostulation with Inigo Jones*

Master Surveyor, you that first began
From thirty pounds in pipkins, to the man
You are: from them leaped forth an architect,
Able to talk of Euclid, and correct
Both him and Archimede. . . .

What is the cause you pomp it so, I ask?
And all men echo, you have made a masque.
I chime that too, and I have met with those
That do cry up the machine and the shows;

The majesty of Juno in the clouds,
And peering forth of Iris in the shrouds;
The ascent of Lady Fame, which none could spy,
Not they that sided her, Dame Poetry,
Dame History, Dame Architecture too,
And Goody Sculpture, brought with much ado
To hold her up: O shows, shows, mighty shows!
The eloquence of masques! what need of prose,
Or verse, or sense, t' express immortal you?
You are the spectacles of state, 'tis true,
Court-hieroglyphics and all arts afford,
In the mere perspective of an inch-board;
You ask no more than certain politic eyes,
Eyes that can pierce into the mysteries
Of many colours, read them and reveal
Mythology, there painted on slit deal.
Or to make boards to speak! there is a task!
Painting and carpentry are the soul of masque.
Pack with your peddling poetry to the stage,
This is the money-got, mechanic age.
To plant the music where no ear can reach,
Attire the persons as no thought can teach
Sense what they are; which by a specious, fine
Term of you architects, is called Design;
But in the practised truth, destruction is
Of any art beside what he calls his. . . .

O wise surveyor, wiser architect,
But wisest Inigo; who can reflect
On the new priming of thy old sign-posts,
Reviving with fresh colours the pale ghosts
Of thy dead standards; or with marvel see
Thy twice conceived, thrice paid for imagery;
And not fall down before it, and confess
Almighty Architecture, who no less
A goddess is than painted cloth, deal board,

Vermilion, lake, or crimson can afford
Expression for; with that unbounded line
Aimed at in thy omnipotent design!

BEN JONSON (1631)

The well-known collaboration between Ben Jonson and Inigo Jones in the production of a series of highly poetic and decorative masques for the Stuart Court, from 1605 onwards, was anything but placid, poet and artist being eternally at loggerheads over the relative importance of their respective roles.

S is for scenery. Gordon Craig and the rest
just hang up a duster and hope for the best

HUMBERT WOLFE (1932)

Scenery

From *The London Theatres*

Who, when the palace and the garden claim
Their breathing statues, who can paint like thee
Impressive tasteful Smirke? . . . How grand how vast
Thy curtain of new Drury, in design,
Judicious Malton! Thy receding scene
Of architectural beauty so deceives,
The eye of admiration that we ask . . .
'Is this majestic view, unreal all?
The rising column and the stately arch
Can ne'er be pictured thus! 'Tis not in art.'
Yes. 'Tis in art. For see, the gathering wind
Give motion to the canvas!

The Loves and Graces crowd the cheerful stage,
And hark! The distant bells, in lively chime,
Fling to the echoing space their pleasing sound.

THOMAS BELLAMY (1795)

Smirke was a celebrated scene painter both at Covent Garden and
Drury Lane, and it is thought he may have been the father of the
famous Sir Robert Smirke, the architect. Malton also worked at the
two major theatres; he was an architectural draughtsman, and
decorative and scenic painter. J M W Turner was a pupil of his, and
later said that Tom Malton had been his 'real master'.

With gilded scenes no drama dares dispense;
But shifters shove them in the place of sense.
Important shifters! Who with painters share
The highest honours of the Thespian chair.

The Thespiad (1809)

Carver, Loutherbourg, and Richards
Scene-Painters to the Theatre Royal, Covent Garden

Though from Thalia's stores I drew my lot,
Should Painting, once my joy, be quite forgot?
Tho' lost to memory thy lovely face,
Come, here amongst my numbers take thy place;
That part of thee, all grand, sublime, serene,
Which to the words and action gives the scene;
What to spectators such new pleasure brings,
From wonders done by *cloudings*, *flats*, and *wings*;
The Painter customs marks, he notes the clime,
And then adapts his scenes to place and time;
Observes what seasons, morning, noon, or night,
Sun-rise, sun-set, and stage devoid of light.

My castle, forest, cavern, undermining,
By Carver painted, Richards' first designing;

A Loutherbourg's bold genius took full range,
Through Cook's South Islands, savage, wild, and strange;
In pieces cut, broad scene that seem'd so nigh,
Thus spreading miles of distance to the eye;
Opaque he made transparent on occasion,
Volcano, sun-set, or a conflagration;
And my *Omai* furnish'd him with scope,
To give a full effect to ardent hope.

JOHN O'KEEFFE (1826)

The Curtains

On the big curtain paint the cantankerous
Peace dove of my brother Picasso. Behind it
Stretch the wire rope and hang
My lightly fluttering half curtains
Which cross like two waves of foam to make
The working woman handing out pamphlets
And the recanting Galileo both disappear.
Following the change of plays they can be
Of rough linen or of silk
Or of white leather or of red, and so on.
Only don't make them too dark, for on them
You must project the titles of the following
Incidents, for the sake of tension and that
The right thing may be expected. And please make
My curtain half-height, don't block the stage off.
Leaning back, let the spectator
Notice the busy preparations being so
Ingeniously made for him, a tin moon is
Seen swinging down, a shingle roof
Is carried in; don't show him too much
But show something. And let him observe
That this is not magic but
Work, my friends.

BERTOLT BRECHT (*c* 1950)
(Trans. John Willett)

The Lighting

Electrician
Give us light on our stage.
How can we disclose
We playwrights and actors
Images to the world in semi-darkness?
The sleepy twilight sends to sleep.
Yet we need our watchers wide awake.
Indeed we need them vigilant.
Let them dream in brightness. The little bit
Of night that's wanted now and then
Our lamps and moons can indicate.
And we with our acting too can keep
The times of day apart.
The Elizabethan wrote us
Verses on a heath at evening
Which no lights will ever reach
Nor even the heath itself embrace.
Therefore flood full on
What we have made with work
That the watcher may see
The indignant peasant
Sit down upon the soil of Tavastland
As though it were her own.

BERTOLT BRECHT (*c* 1950)
(Trans. John Willett)

Limelight

I work the limes,
  And there are times
When sittin' on my ladder of a night,
  I try an' try
To find the reason why
A Star wants hextry light.

  I've worked the limes
  In pantomimes
An' done a gradual change from mauve to white.
  The same old game –
Miss Tottie What's-'er-name,
The Star, wants hall the light!

  I've throwed a lime
  Right on a crime
Wot should have been committed out of sight.
  The scene was billed:
'Hin darkness 'e was killed' –
Hexcuse for hextry light.

  I work them limes
  As Poet rhymes –
No heffort – it's a gift – like happetite.
  But still it jars
To think that certain Stars
Wants hartificial light.

ALBERT CHEVALIER (1903)

A Sonnet

Only connect! Should be the motto of your trade
Which, silently, invisibly, you ply behind the scenes.
Without your sparking power no play is played,
No shafts illuminate this stuff of dreams.
Where is that neutral being live on earth
Who could deny one socket to your plug?
Since you enable us to conjure mirth,
Or weave sad tales that at the heart-strings tug?

He who elects to serve thus, ne'er applauded,
Whate'er his shade, blue, brown, or yellow-green,
Shall in the actors' memories be lauded
For by your light alone we all are seen.
O! May you feel your efforts have been worth it,
When Death shall come; the ultimate Short-Circuit.

ALISON SKILBECK (1982)

The Fascination of What's Difficult

The fascination of what's difficult
Has dried the sap out of my veins, and rent
Spontaneous joy and natural content
Out of my heart. There's something ails our colt
That must, as if it had not holy blood
Nor on Olympus leaped from cloud to cloud,
Shiver under the lash, strain, sweat and jolt
As though it dragged road metal. My curse on plays
That have to be set up in fifty ways,
On the day's war with every knave and dolt,
Theatre business, management of men.
I swear before the dawn comes round again
I'll find the stable and pull out the bolt.

W B YEATS (1910)

Prosaic Justice

She said a good Company Manager
should be in an hour before the half.
I ought to have told her to fault-find
only when I had done something wrong.

She was usually here by now.
I wandered to prompt corner,
asked the DSM if he'd called her.

I started to move towards the double swing-doors
– no sign. I couldn't hear her on the stairs,
so I ran to the second-floor dressing-room,
knocked, went straight in –
she was fast asleep on her sofa.

I shook her, she gave a startled gasp.
'You're on' – horror seized her,
she flew off the sofa
into her shoes, down the corridor,
met somebody on the stairs –
her shoe came off, she picked it up,
ran with it in her hand.

Through the swing-doors
into the wings, heard the line
before her entrance, jumped into bed,
set the shoes, said 'Thank you Malcolm'
in the calmest imaginable voice,
as the bedroom revolved onto the stage.

That'll teach her for trying to tell me
I was inefficient yesterday.

MALCOLM WROE (1987)

Under the Stage

We opened up the stage today.
Two flat traps resting hingeless
over a black depth of forty feet
which sucked at our legs and arms
as we handled the deadwood
four-ply in a shuffle.
John came up with two ladders
and laid them across the spot,
splayed their legs on their sides
as fear changed our minds
about the day, in gibberish.
'Any actor wouldn't put a foot
here would he if he knew.'

But we do.
And we walk over it
and over it until
it all falls through.
Something living
under the stage
breathes us in.

MICHAEL FOLEY (1978)

The Scene-Shifter

I takes hoff my 'at to one bloke, an' to 'im alone –
      Don't know 'is name –
Seen pickshurs of 'im tho' a-liftin' on 'is own
      The world – nice bloomin' game!
I've 'ad the Tah'r of London hon my back
      An' the Ahse of Lords as well –
      Got fined, because I fell! –
        That's a bit of 'orlright,' ain' it?

Why! I've pulled dahn 'aunted castles wivaht spade or pick!
  I 'ave – that's straight,
Hall on my lonesome, too – in less than 'arf a tick –
  I 'ave – an' let me state,
I've shoved the 'ole of 'yde Park hin its place –
   Squashed it into thirty feet,
   No 'ank! That's 'ard to beat –
    It's a bit of 'orlright,' ain' it?

I've packed Paris and the Alps away, with Rome on top,
   An' still I'm here! –
You take a tip from me, it ain't no fancy 'cop,'
   You bet it ain't – no fear!
Why these 'ere 'ands 'as lifted hup the sea!
   Yuss! Think of that an' weep –
   The bloomin' briny deep! –
    That's a bit of 'orlright,' ain' it?

      ALBERT CHEVALIER (1903)

Nothing Unusual about Today

The Master Carpenter too drunk to stand
was sleeping in the wings.
The first cue done by Peter
(nicknamed the simple) was slow.
The Master Carpenter, now awake,
said he would turn the revolve faster.

He was true to his word.
He spilled two actors onto the stage
in the blackout, also
he had taken the revolve the wrong way.
Immediately he took it back –
like a humming top –
tipping the other actors backstage.
They were not pleased.

      MALCOLM WROE (1987)

'Noises Off'

From the Prologue to *Every Man in his Humour*

Nor creaking throne comes down, the boys to please;
Nor nimble squib is seen, to make afear'd
The gentlewomen; nor rolled bullet heard
To say, it thunders; nor tempestuous drum
Rumbles to tell you when the storm doth come.

BEN JONSON (1598)

To be Sold by Auction

In *The Life of an Actor* by Pierce Egan

To be Sold by Auction,
By Messrs PRATTLE and HAMMERALL,
a very magnificent and improving
THEATRICAL PROPERTY,
including all the
LIVE AND DEAD STOCK OF
PUPPETS *and* PIGMIES, MUSIC, WARDROBE,
WHISKERS, WIGS, *and* INNUMERABLE GIM-CRACKS
and NICKNACATORIES:
Together with a
Stock MOON in all its Quarters,
Hail, Rain, Wind, Sleet, and
overwhelming *Torrents* of all sorts.
THERE WILL ALSO BE FOUND
among this inestimable property (which was never
before heard of, and never will be again), a great
variety of
STATUES, GARDENS, WATER WORKS
(*not real*)
CASTLES *and* MANSIONS, most delightfully
situated,

ALSO
GROVES, WOODS, FORESTS, and PASTEBOARD COUNTRY
SEATS, pleasantly wooded on all sides,
Many miles from the *Metropolis*, and consequently
no *prospect* of his Majesty's seat, vulgarly called
the *King's Bench*.

BEING THE MOVEABLES OF
Messrs T A G and G A G,
WHOSE FORTUNES
have been ruined in the COUNTRY, by the Successes
of their Relatives in TOWN,
THE WHOLE OF WHICH
will be positively disposed of, without
RESERVE, PREFERENCE, *or* REFERENCE
On MONDAY *next*, June 17, 1823.

———

THE INVENTORY

ONE shower of snow, in the whitest French paper,
Two ditto in brown, if the white should get taper;
One dozen of clouds, edges trimm'd with black crape;
A ditto (French set) of a more rotund shape,
Streak'd with lightning, and varnish'd with lamp-lighter's
    oil,
And gilt on the edges, touch'd up with brass foil;
One cauldron; a skull; a magician's black kettle;
A rainbow complete, only faded a little;
A Momus's staff; Squire Hawthorn's stock gun;
An assortment of stones, and a fine setting sun;
Some poisons mix'd up, and quite ready for use;
A champanzee's dress for the ape in *Perouse*;
A mantle (imperial) for Cyrus the Great,
Worn by Caesar and others, when seated in state;
One sword (basket hilt) lined with rose-colour'd silk,
And handy, when done with, to take in the milk;
A dozen of rattles; a pair of large globes;

And part of a king's coronation mock robes;
A trick pot of porter; a pantomime pig;
The whiskers of *Blue Beard*, mustachios and wig;
The throne of an Indian, surmounted with palm;
Six waves in a tempest; six ditto, when calm;
Roxana's best helmet, with gold cord well bound;
Othello's lost handkerchief, lately been found;
Three goats and a parrot for *Robinson Crusoe*;
Some wind, that so loud is, the real never blew so;
Two streamlets, and painted effect to produce,
Real water, at that time, was never in use;
A serpent, to sting Cleopatra's fair arm,
And four masks that the devil himself might alarm;
Some roses in foil, that to gather might tempt ye;
A file full of bills, and a treasury empty;
A troop of young horse, which, 'tis said on their labels,
Were as yet never fed in Bill Davies's stables;
A dragon; a giantess; eight pasteboard kings;
A large tarnished lyre, without any strings;
A group of young angels; six devils in black;
A crowbar for Romeo: a wheel and a rack;
Six sickles for reapers; a cowl for a monk;
An assassin's complexion, packed up in a trunk,
Consisting of cork, burnt as black as a cinder,
And a woolly dark scalp, but as rotten as tinder;
A stone colour'd suit, fit for any stock ghost;
One turnpike, one mile stone, and trick finger post;
Two new pilgrim's staffs; set of beads for a friar;
And two feet six inches of transparent fire;
A plume of white feathers, not worn above thrice
By Tybalt, but nibbled a bit by the mice;
Swords of various forms, pikes, cardinals' hats,
Lightning boxes, sheep hooks, and three harlequin's bats;
A gibbet once made for the famed *Siege of Calais*,
Though a wag had wrote on it, in ill-natured malice,
'This lot will be bought in, an excellent plan,
For the manager's use, or perhaps for his man;'

A file of old play bills, which might do to bind,
With only the play for next night – underlined;
When a single sheet bill was considered enough,
Ere managers built less on talent than PUFF!
Two manuscript dramas, 'twas said wouldn't do,
At the fourth page turned down, and so never read through;
But why not return them again to the poet?
But that's not the fashion, and poor AUTHORS know it.
When they've taken from pieces those things which will
    strike,
The owners may have them again, – if they like!
These things your attention most richly deserve,
And each lot will be sold without any reserve;
To the friends of Virtu, in the unique and curious,
They'll afford a rich treat, as they're vouch'd – as not
    spurious.
The 'effects' will be 'put up' next Monday at two,
Till when, all the lots will remain upon view,
The purchaser then must pay down a deposit,
As the 'Sale' will take place – in the PROPERTY CLOSET.

T GREENWOOD (1825)

The Wardrobe Mistress

Saddened by dreams of what she might have been,
    Sick with the thought of what she is to-day,
    She droops, a little woman, pinched and gray,
Within the shadow of a painted scene;
Still lingers on her weary face the sheen
    Of make-believe; the cruel crow's-feet stray
    Beneath her faded eyes, and mute dismay
Lurks in her timid and pathetic mien.

213

Echoes of by-gone triumphs wake her breast –
   The nights of tinselled bliss, the dizzy whirl,
   The sparkling gauds, the limelight and the band –
   Now with a needle in her work-worn hand,
She potters round the wings, all drably drest,
Stitching the trappings of some thoughtless girl.

JOHN FERGUSON (1912)

The Dresser

I 'elp 'im wiv 'is props
    An' turn 'im aht
    Hall spick an' span.
I likes occaish'nal drops
    Of special staht –
    I'm but a man;
An' 'e's a star – a dror on hany bill.

But where'd 'e be, I'd arst,
    Hif 'umble I
    Cleared hoff one night?
The worm may turn at larst
    An' do a guy
    To scenes more bright;
An' wander far – I don't say that it will.

'E ain't not bad at 'eart –
    'Ot-'eaded tho!
    An' 'asty too.
'E couldn't play 'is part
    If I did go –
    A nice ter-do!
The bloomin' 'unt for props 'u'd queer 'is 'ealf.

Oh! 'e can act orlright
    Wiv 'elp, of course,
    From hexpert 'and.
Hif I should go, 'e might
    P'raps feel the loss;
    An' understand
When 'e'd ter shunt, an' dress 'is bloomin' self!

'E torks abaht 'is nerves! –
    An' wot price mine?
    Fair shook ter bits! –
I scornfully observes;
    Hall very fine,
    'E don't 'ave fits
Or fall dahn flat. 'E's well enough, bar fads!

Suppose 'e 'eard me talk?
    Well, s'pose 'e did.
    'E'd just say 'Jack,
You'd better take a walk
    An' stop that kid!'
    Give me the sack?
No fear of that! I'd blow the gaff! – 'e pads!!

ALBERT CHEVALIER (1903)

Old Age Make-Up

The actor in his dressing-room

'Nightly I sit for a couple of hours
Watching the face in my mirror age:
Putty puffing and flabbing my cheeks,
Patched and blotched thready blood-vessel
Bags and wrinkles thumbed into the putty;
Stuffing to pad my stomach and arse;

Wig to dissolve my curly red hair
Into grey wisps on a nude skin dome.
I drop the spectacles on my rheumy nose,
Attach the cord of my hearing-aid,
And shuffle, stick-propped, out to the lights
To earn my salary for the presentation
Of nature's vilest obscenity – age.

'Three hours later I watch for my face,
Pallid with spirits and cleaning-oils,
To emerge from the blotches and skin-sag.
                                        Each night
I try to give thanks for the miracle
Which throws away my stick, my specs,
My hearing-aid at the curtain call,
Remembering the millions of innocent clowns,
Who, like the mask-swapping mime with the wrong
Mask stuck to his terrified face, are trapped
With old age puttied on their skin for keeps.'

LEO AYLEN (1983)

The Call-Boy

With all the pride that's born of brief command
        He calls "alf hour!'
The tone is unimpassioned, bold, but bland,
        "Alf hour! 'alf hour!'
            He stands for Time,
            His voice the chime:
                'Alf hour! 'alf hour!'

You badly need a final look through, so
    The chance you seize;
But moments fly, and soon he lets you know:
    'The quarter, please!'
        Say what you will,
        It sends a thrill:
           'The quarter, please!'

You hear the bandsmen tuning up downstairs –
    A ghastly row!
Your state of mind the madd'ning muddle shares,
    Chaotic now.
        'What is my cue?
        Shall I pull through?
           And if so – how?'

The flutes and fiddles practise dismal scales
    In different keys;
But through the din one clarion voice prevails:
    'Beginners, please!'
        O'er horns and flutes
        The warning shoots:
           'Beginners, please!'

The curtain's up at last. It's getting near.
    You wish your knees
Were just a trifle steadier – then, oh! dear!
    'Your call, sir, please!'
        It's time to go
        Or queer the show:
           'Your call, sir, please!'

The curtain's down. You think it's over when
    They play 'The Queen.'
But no! 'To-morrow, sir, you're called at ten,
    They've cut your scene!'
        'My scene? . . . Don't chaff!
        What! – more than half?'
          'They've cut it – *clean*!'

ALBERT CHEVALIER (1903)

Superstitions

And of Macbeth, speak nothing,
Nor his name, nor his play, nor
Its last line, no last line of any play,
For it signifies completion, nothing.
No whistle in the dressing-room. It indicates
Short-run, return to nothing.
No real flowers on stage. They slip,
The actor slides, his part is gone,
He is nothing.
No green doublet in the play. The limelight
Cancels the colour and the actor is nothing.
Peacock's feathers are too distracting.
None sees the actor. He is nothing.
And of nothing, nothing will come.
Shadows on the boards
Are shadows of nothing.

JONATHAN FIELD (1990)

'The Prompter'

I

Whether from want of diligence perplexed,
Or scorning closely to repeat your text,
Your utmost talents hence you never reach,
Your mind's abstracted to rehearse your speech;
And while confused the hiss alone you hear
The louder prompt offends the public ear.

The Prompter (1810)

2

My importance is nil on the hundredth night when the
　actors know their words,
When hearts are not fluttering uncontrolled like so many
　frightened birds.
It's a different thing on a première though: I am somebody
　then indeed,
And many a veteran's found me a friend in the moment of
　direst need. . . .

If they stick for a line – which they often do, – and they
　don't catch what I say,
I look, when they tackle me afterwards, the picture of blank
　dismay.
I just 'kid' they appeared so serenely cool that I didn't
　observe the slip,
Then they hint that I needn't tell anyone else – and I always
　take a tip!

ALBERT CHEVALIER (1903)

3

'Tis the voice of the actor,
  I heard him complain,
'You have prompted too soon,
  So don't prompt me again.

'Never prompt actors
  Till the prompting is due.
If you can't get it right,
  Wait for *me* to prompt *you*.'

JONATHAN FIELD (1990)

Going Round Afterwards

His face was orange.
His widow's peak had been blacked in.
I knew it was him,
because he didn't speak.
'Congratulations!' I said.
'I didn't know you could cry.'
His dresser was holding
a pair of check trousers
underneath his chin. He let the legs
drop through a coathanger
and smiled at me deafly.
'It's just a trick,' said my father.
'Anyone can do it.'
I stood there with my drink,
feeling the ingenious glamour
of being cramped, the mild delinquency
of things behind curtains –
shirts and cardigans
that should have been at home.
Did I have the guts?
And did you have to want it all that much
in order to go on?

His face came up from the wash basin
white and unwell again,
a trace of make-up underneath his ears.
His dresser was handing him
another pair of trousers,
holding them up off the floor
as my father stepped into them.

HUGO WILLIAMS (1985)

The Green Room

Say, where does the murd'rer make
    His victim roar with laughter
    When, talking of it after,
He mentions some mistake –
    Some trifling slip,
    Some whisper'd quip,
Which might have made his awful crime
Seem anything but tragic, at the time?

Say, where does a heroine look,
    With loving eyes up-lifted,
    At villain, strangely gifted –
At one, who erstwhile shook
    With passion's storm –
    Who seized her form,
And frightened her some thirty seconds back
By swearing he was 'still upon her track'?

Say, where does the Jester creep,
    The glare and tinsel shunning,
    While laughter at his punning
Still echoes loud and deep?
    I know a place,
    Where painted face
Cannot disguise the pallor of the soul –
Where tragedy is not denied the Droll.

ALBERT CHEVALIER (1903)

Curtain

When Vyo-Lyn have come and gone
and Queen Zudora's act is over
and Violet's leopard turn is done
and Felice runs to meet her lover

when cards and wands are laid away
and music stops and people hurry
and the dying man for one more day
postpones the fever and the worry

then, when the birds in hooded cage
are perched in silent rows and sleeping,
the redfaced stage-hand takes the stage,
and noisily goes across it, sweeping

the dust of golden-slippered feet,
spangles, and scraps of rainbow paper,
where Rose or Lily sang so sweet,
and Frost or Coffin cut a caper,

and having swept, turns out the lights,
and knocks his pipe, and leaves the curtain
hung high and dark for other nights,
and other vain things just as certain.

CONRAD AIKEN (*c* 1960)

Elegy in a Theatrical Warehouse

They have laid the penthouse scenes away, after a truly
    phenomenal run,
And taken apart the courtroom, and the bright, shiny office,
    and laid them all away with the cabin in the clearing,
    where the sun slowly rose through a smashing third act.
And the old family mansion on the road above the mill has
    been gone a long time
And the road is gone,
The road that never did lead to any mill at all.

The telephone is gone, the phone that rang and rang and
    never did connect with any other phone,
And the great steel safe, where no diamonds ever were.
They have taken down the pictures, portraits of ancestors
    lost and unclaimed, that hung on the massive walls,
And taken away the books that reached the study ceiling,
The rooms and rooms of books bound in leather and gold,
    with nothing, nothing, nothing inside
And the bureaux and the chests that were empty to the
    brim,
And the pistols that brought down so many, many curtains
    with so many, many blanks
Almost everything is gone,
Everything that never held a single thing at all.

KENNETH FEARING (1943)

223

THE BUSINESS

Sad happy race! Soon raised and soon depress'd,
Your days all pass'd in jeopardy and jest.

GEORGE CRABBE (1810)

An Actor's Life

A Song from *The Bohemians*

If I might choose my destiny
An Actor's lot be mine!
For half a dozen other lives
With his own life combine.

Tho' he's poor by Fortune's malice,
And tho' his coat be bare and old,
Night bestows a regal palace,
And he'll robe, in cloth of gold!

    Such is the players' magic story,
    Passing quick from grave to gay,
    Up and down,
    Rags and crown,
    Rich tomorrow poor today.

If larder lack, or cellar fail
What actor should repine?
He quaffs an empty cup
And on a wooden joint can dine!

Actors too can flourish after
The dagger sharp, the poison bowl!
Groaning's kill'd by sudden laughter
While a jolly song they'll troll!

    Such is the players' magic story,
    Passing quick from grave to gay,
    Up and down,
    Rags and crown,
    In the self–same day!

H B FARNIE (c 1870)

The Strolling Tribe

From *The Apology*

The strolling tribe, a despicable race,
Like wand'ring Arabs, shift from place to place. . . .

In shabby state they strut, and tatter'd robe,
The scene a blanket, and a barn the globe.
No high conceits their mod'rate wishes raise,
Content with humble profit, humble praise.
Let dowdies simper, and let bumpkins stare,
The strolling pageant hero treads in air:
Pleas'd for his hour he to mankind gives law,
And snores the next out on a truss of straw.

CHARLES CHURCHILL (1761)

Players

From *The Borough*

Drawn by the annual call, we now behold
Our troop dramatic, heroes known of old,
And those, since last they march'd, inlisted and enroll'd:
Mounted on hacks or borne in waggons some,
The rest on foot (the humbler brethren) come.
Three favour'd places, an unequal time,
Join to support this company sublime:
Ours for the longer period – see how light
Yon parties move, their former friends in sight,
Whose claims are all allow'd, and friendship glads the night.
Now public rooms shall sound with words divine,
And private lodgings hear how heroes shine;
No talk of pay shall yet on pleasure steal,
But kindest welcome bless the friendly meal;
While o'er the social jug and decent cheer,
Shall be described the fortune of the year.

Peruse these bills, and see what each can do.
Behold! The prince, the slave, the monk, the Jew;
Change but the garment, and they'll all engage
To take each part, and act in every age:
Cull'd from all houses, what a house are they!
Swept from all barns, our borough-critics say;
But with some portion of a critic's ire,
We all endure them; there are some admire:
They might have praise, confined to farce alone;
Full well they grin, they should not try to groan;
But then our servants' and our seamen's wives
Love all that rant and rapture as their lives;
He who Squire Richard's part could well sustain,
Finds as King Richard he must roar amain –
'My horse! My horse!' Lo! Now to their abodes,
Come lords and lovers, empresses and gods.

The master-mover of these scenes has made
No trifling gain in this adventurous trade;
Trade we may term it, for he duly buys
Arms out of use and undirected eyes;
These he instructs, and guides them as he can,
And vends each night the manufactured man:
Long as our custom lasts, they gladly stay,
Then strike their tents, like Tartars, and away!
The place grows bare where they too long remain,
But grass will rise ere they return again.

Children of Thespis, welcome! Knights and queens!
Counts! Barons! Beauties! When before your scenes,
And mighty monarchs thund'ring from your throne;
Then step behind, and all your glory's gone:
Of crown and palace, throne and guards bereft,
The pomp is vanish'd, and the care is left.
Yet strong and lively is the joy they feel,
When the full house secures the plenteous meal;
Flatt'ring and flatter'd, each attempts to raise
A brother's merits for a brother's praise:

For never hero shows a prouder heart,
Than he who proudly acts a hero's part;
Nor without cause; the boards, we know, can yield
Place for fierce contest, like the tented field.

Graceful to tread the stage, to be in turn
The prince we honour, and the knave we spurn;
Bravely to bear the tumult of the crowd,
The hiss tremendous, and the censure loud:
These are their parts, – and he who these sustains
Deserves some praise and profit for his pains.
Heroes at least of gentler kind are they,
Against whose swords no weeping widows pray,
No blood their fury sheds, nor havoc marks their way.

Sad happy race! Soon raised and soon depress'd,
Your days all pass'd in jeopardy and jest;
Poor without prudence, with afflictions vain,
Not warn'd by misery, not enrich'd by gain;
Whom justice pitying, chides from place to place,
A wandering, careless, wretched, merry race,
Who cheerful looks assume, and play the parts
Of happy rovers with repining hearts;
Then cast off care, and in the mimic pain
Of tragic woe, feel spirits light and vain,
Distress and hope – the mind's, the body's wear,
The man's affliction, and the actor's tear:
Alternate times of fasting and excess
Are yours, ye smiling children of distress.

Slaves though ye be, your wandering freedom seems,
And with your varying views and restless schemes,
Your griefs are transient, as your joys are dreams.
Yet keen those griefs – ah! What avail thy charms,
Fair Juliet! What that infant in thine arms

What those heroic lines thy patience learns
What all the aid thy present Romeo earns,
Whilst thou art crowded in that lumbering wain,
With all thy plaintive sisters to complain?
Nor is there lack of labour: to rehearse,
Day after day, poor scraps of prose and verse
To bear each other's spirit, pride, and spite
To hide in rant the heart-ache of the night
To dress in gaudy patch-work, and to force
The mind to think on the appointed course –
This is laborious, and may be defined
The bootless labour of the thriftless mind.

GEORGE CRABBE (1810)

'Train Call'

Lines to the rhythm of a well-known poem

Oh! the long and dreary touring
Oh! rehearsals under Wolfit
Oh! the packing and unpacking
And the laundry calls on Monday
Sigh the staff and sigh the actors
Groan the worn-out wardrobe baskets
Little baskets – worn with travel
What another play this autumn
Are there more plays still by Shakespeare
Has he got a sleeve – what's up it
Mighty tourer – ruddy nuisance!
Then up spake old Brownlow comic.
Skipping gaily up the staircase
Throwing walking sticks from off him
Come my children this is touring

231

Railway journeys lie before us
And there is great reservation
Special coaches for the actors
And kind foremen on the railways
Who will see you miss connections
Put your coaches in the sidings
Where you'll sleep in great discomfort.

DONALD WOLFIT (1943)

'Success'

From *The Return from Parnassus*

England affords these glorious vagabonds,
That carried erst their fardles on their backs,
Coursers to ride on through the gazing streets,
Sweeping it in their glaring satin suits,
And pages to attend their masterships:
With mouthing words, that better wits have framed,
They purchase lands, and now esquires are made.

ANON (*c* 1600)

'Unfair Competition'

From Praeludium for *The Careless Shepherdess*

. . . The Court, and Inns of Court,
Of late bring forth more wit than all the taverns,
Which makes me pity playwrights; they were poor
Before, even to a proverb; now their trade
Must needs go down, when so many set up.
I do not think but I shall shortly see
One poet sue to keep the door, another
To be prompter, a third to snuff the candles.

ANON (*c* 1638)

'Bard Equals Box Office'

So have I seen, when Caesar would appear,
And on the stage at half-sword parley were
Brutus and Cassius: oh how the audience
Were ravish'd, with what wonder they went thence;
When some new day they would not brook a line
Of tedious (though well laboured) Catiline;
Sejanus too was irksome, they priz'd more
Honest Iago, or the jealous Moor.
And though Fox and the subtle Alchemist,
Long intermitted, could not quite be miss'd, . . .

Yet these sometimes, even at a friend's desire
Acted, have scarce defray'd the sea-coal fire
And door-keepers; when but let Falstaff come,
All is so pester'd; let but Beatrice
And Benedick be seen, lo in a trice
The Cockpit galleries, boxes, all are full
To hear Malvolio, that cross garter'd gull.

LEONARD DIGGES (1623)

A Visit to Stratford

And was he innocent as you protest
Of these hot wheels, this tide, this trade, this sawdust?
No, there was weakness in him that foreknew,
Even claimed it with a brazen *non sans droict*,
And here's his pedigree which pardon me
I do not mean to read, *found in his closet.*
His rival playwrights laughed and nudged at this
For patronage busy among the heralds
In gratitude for secret service rendered
Had cut all tangled genealogic knots
And sealed the lie – linking the generations
We also laugh at him, in spite of love,

To go no further than the tanner's son.
The tannery failed, beginning the long turmoil:
Turmoil brought settled grief, grief, fear of death:
This fear postponed itself in architecture:
Architecture spelt itself sweet death;
After death the abstraction of the body
(Protected by the merest formal curse)
Freeing the massy tomb for commendation,
For commentaries, for mere scholiasm:
And scholiasm bred strange heresies
Which thinned and spread in chatter through the schools:
Chatter brought pilgrims flocking, therefore trade:
Trade, this false history, this word-worn patter:
So, timber from the mulberry that he planted
Miraculously multiplied, enough
To plank and roof a great memorial hall
For summer festivals: his eight least plays,
The *Shrew* and *Merry Wives* starring the bill:
Matinees, Saturdays and Wednesdays: stalls
And sideshows valeted by the Concordance.
Oh, he foreknew the frequence of the sequence –
Sixpence a ticket, sixpence, sixpence,
School-children with their teachers, twopence.
The hackney rides, quotation to quotation,
To be or not to be. The bubble reputation.
A grievous fault (for one so rich of wit)
And grievously has Caesar answered it.

ROBERT GRAVES (*c* 1925)

Sacred Fire

Is Shakespeare dead?
If so why is everybody heading for the River Avon?
bringing their diversity of tongues
to a hover over a theatre;
to the conversion of local tour operators
into missionaries.

All tourism this, to the horror of street-corner prophets
who mea culpa madly
in their stance
these crowmen —— pretenders to a robbery of sacred fire.

Who needs proof of faith with all these feet?
So roll back the stone!
Who is dead where here are
blackbooks promptbooks
cleanhands stagehands
actors who sing 'We aim to please you' and this
ranter who screams that few are chosen

who rends the air with proof like local storms
who slaps bricks with holy vowels
who echoes blacksuit howls
of wings, haloes and flaming swords
till death comes by facelessness
a kind of baptism in Stratford-on-Avon
for drowning street-corner prophets
unable to keep up with the rate of dollars and cents.

And Shakespeare is chosen –
his tomb is in the church above
his name on every Stratford door
yea, and his monument there, before the bridge
and born in Henley Street. Amen

While inside, an audience wash with the sound of their
    hands
after witnessing a show of unseen power
transubstantiated actors, flats and follow spots;
an audience who men and women not for rumours
let their pilgrimage go climax in applause.

MICHAEL FOLEY (1974)

Shakespeare (whom you and ev'ry Play-house bill
Style the divine, the matchless, what you will)
For gain, not glory, wing'd his roving flight,
And grew Immortal, in his own despite.

ALEXANDER POPE (1737)

'At the Box-Office'

From Praeludium for *The Careless Shepherdess*

(BOLT, *a Door-keeper, sitting with a Box on one side of the Stage.
    To him* THRIFT, *a Citizen.*)

THRIFT: Now for a good bargain. What will you take
To let me in to the play? BOLT: A shilling Sir.

THRIFT: Come, here's a groat, I'll not make many words,
Thou hast just got my trick for all the world,
I always use to ask just twice as much
As a thing's worth: then some pretend to have
Skill in my wares, by bidding of me half.
But when I meet a man of judgement, as
You have done now, they bid as near to th' price,
As if they knew my mark. Use me, as you
Do hope to have my custom other times.

236

BOLT: In troth Sir I can't take it. THRIFT: Should I go
Away, I know you'd call me back again.
I hate this dodging: what's your lowest price?

BOLT: I told you at first word. THRIFT: What, a shilling?
Why, I have known some Aldermen that did
Begin with twelve pence; and for half so much
I saw six motions last Bartholomew Fair.

BOLT: When you have seen this play, you'll think it worth
Your money. THRIFT: Well then take this groat in earnest,
If I do like it you shall have the rest.

BOLT: This is no market or exchange, pray keep
Your airy groat that's thinner than a shadow,
To mend your worship's shoes, it is more crack'd
Than an old beaver or a chambermaid.

THRIFT: Well, since you will exact, and stretch your
    conscience,
Here's a nine-pence and four-pence half-penny,
Give me the rest again. BOLT: There!

ANON (*c* 1638)

. . . Those that come to see
    Only a show or two, and so agree
    The play may pass, if they be still and willing,
    I'll undertake may see away their shilling
    Richly in two short hours.

WILLIAM SHAKESPEARE (1613)

King John in a Cocked Hat,
or Heigh Ho Says Kemble

A parody on the famous Grimaldian song
The Frog in the Opera Hat

John Kemble he would an–acting go,
   Heigho! says Kemble;
He rais'd the price which he thought too low,
Whether the public would let him or no;
     With his roly–poly, gammon, and spinnage.
   And ho! says manager Kemble.

The mob at the door made a mighty din,
   Heigho! says Kemble;
They dash'd like devils thro' thick and thin,
And over the benches came tumbling in,
     With their roly–poly, gammon and spinnage,
   'Twill do, says manager Kemble.

Soon as they pass'd Bill Shakespeare's hall,
   Heigho! says Kemble;
They thought the lobbies were much too small,
So they gave a loud roar and they gave a loud bawl,
     With roly–poly, gammon and spinnage,
   Hello! says manager Kemble.

Pray *what do you want?* (in a sort of a huff)
   Heigho! says Kemble;
Says Mr Leigh, 'Nonsensical stuff!
Pho! None of your gammon, you know well enough,
     With your roly–poly, gammon and spinnage,
   You do, great manager Kemble.'

He held by the tip his opera-hat,
   Heigho! says Kemble;
Indeed the concern's as poor as a rat;
Says Bull, 'No, damme, we won't stand that!
     With our roly-poly, gammon and spinnage,
   'Twon't do, great manager Kemble.'

He folded his arms in a sad nonplus,
   Heigho! says Kemble;
With Queen Anne's prices he made a fuss,
Says Bull, 'What the devil's Queen Anne to us?
     With roly-poly, gammon and spinnage,
   'Twon't do, great manager Kemble.'

He swore to himself an oath, by Styx,
   Heigho! says Kemble;
Kind ladies and gentlemen, none of your tricks,
I love seven shillings much better than six,
     With my roly-poly, gammon and spinnage,
   I do, says manager Kemble.

Then roar'd the gallery, gentle souls,
   Heigho! says Kemble;
'No private boxes, no pigeon-holes,
We'll dowse your glims, in a crack, by goles!
     With roly-poly, gammon and spinnage.'
   No, don't! says manager Kemble.

I can't these private boxes rob,
   Heigho! says Kemble;
With Lord O'Straddle I drink hob and nob,
And I'm hand in glove with my Lord Thingumbob;
     With his roly-poly, gammon, and spinnage,
   Good night! says manager Kemble.

                    ANON (1809)

When in 1808 the Theatre Royal, Covent Garden, was burnt down
(for the second time in its history), John Kemble, then its manager,

commissioned a grand and very expensive theatre in its place from the fashionable architect Robert Smirke. To recoup the fortune Kemble had spent on it, he increased the number of private boxes, raised seat prices, and abolished the old shilling gallery altogether. The outraged public replied with the OP (Old Price) Riots. Every night for two months after the opening, the audience hooted, hissed, chanted, displayed placards, wore OP buttons and hats, and danced a special OP dance on the benches of the pit. The ballad printed below was sung nightly in the theatre to the tune of *God Save the King*. In the end Kemble had to give in and restore the shilling gallery.

National Air

Humbly submitted to the Placarding Committee

A Street Ballad

God save Great Johnny Bull,
Long live our noble Bull;
God save John Bull.
Send him victorious,
Loud, and uproarious,
With lungs like Boreas,
God save John Bull.

O Johnny Bull be true,
Oppose the Prices New,
And make them fall.
Curse Kemble's politics,
Frustrate his knavish tricks,
On thee, our hopes we fix,
Confound them all.

No private boxes let
Intriguing ladies get;
Thy right, John Bull.
From little Pigeon Holes,
Defend us jolly souls,
And we will sing, by Goles,
God save John Bull.

ANON (1809)

Hughes
Treasurer to Covent Garden Theatre

Works which the poet's fame must sink or raise,
Excited nor his censure nor his praise.
Yet critics shrewd, and managers, must say,
None better knew the value of a play.
He drew his knowledge, not from Shakespeare's school,
But judg'd by wise Sam Butler's simple rule.
Nor smiles nor frowns to actor or to bard –
He gave, as runs our world, that best reward,
Which bids the grumbling vintner's tongue lie still,
And of its terrors robs the tailor's bill.
Now, tho' his body moulder in the grave,
Let's hope his thoughts and acts his soul may save.
No *charges of the night*; no nightly pay;
Remit his charges, Heaven, in nightless day!

JOHN O'KEEFFE (1826)

'The Advertising Tribe'

From *The Newspaper*

I sing of News, and all those vapid sheets
The rattling hawker vends through gaping streets;
Whate'er their name, whate'er the time they fly,
Damp from the press, to charm the reader's eye:
For, soon as morning dawns with roseate hue,
The Herald of the morn arises too;
Post after Post succeeds, and, all day long,
Gazettes and Ledgers swarm, a noisy throng. . . .

By the same aid, the Stage invites her friends,
And kindly tells the banquet she intends;
Thither from real life the many run,
With Siddons weep, or laugh with Abingdon;
Pleased in fictitious joy or grief, to see
The mimic passion with their own agree;
To steal a few enchanted hours away
From care, and drop the curtain on the day.

GEORGE CRABBE (1785)

Dorkin's Night

A Street Ballad

'Twas Dorkin's night, and the house was a sight,
It was packed from the floor to the roof;
His old friends were there, as they annually were
When their friendship was put to the proof;
And the welcoming shout, which from thousands rang out,
As their favourite came from the wing,
Convinced him, he still could command them at will,
And their laughter or tears could bring.

But they knew not the pain in the poor player's breast
As he strutted and mimicked and smiled;
That while from his lips fell the mirth-giving jest,
He thought of his poor dying child.

The first act was o'er and a deafening roar,
Of cheering went heartily round;
The second act passed! But, alas! In the last,
Dorkin scarcely could utter a sound;
They saw with dismay he was spoiling the play,
It was plain there was something amiss:
And the unfeeling wit of the gods and the pit,
Came at last to a palpable hiss.

But they knew not, &c.

He started! Turned pale, and his form seemed to quail,
But he came to the footlights and spoke;
And the listening house was as still as a mouse,
When the silence he falt'ringly broke:
'My little one's dead, I had left him in bed,
Nearly gone when this drama began;
Yet I hoped he would live. You will surely forgive,
For an actor can be but a man.'

But they knew not, &c.

ANON (1800s)

Ring Down the Curtain

From a Song

Ring down the curtain, I can't sing tonight!
My heart is breaking amid all this light.
My little one's dying, my pride and delight.
So ring down the curtain, I can't sing tonight!

ANON (1902)

On a Chorus Girl

With half a score of singing girls she swings
   Down the bright stage; sustains a rigid pose,
   Toe-dances till her carmine beauty glows,
Then trips into the darkness of the wings:
Changes her dress; and while some 'starlet' sings,
   Into the footlights' glare again she goes,
   Creeps on all fours, and dances on her toes . . .
Her rouged companions do the self-same things.

Twice nightly thus, for thirty bob a week!
   No high Ambition swells her kindly heart,
   No splendid role she craves, no brainy part,
     Yet Hope burns where those spangly sequins shine;
Hope that to her may come the chance to speak –
   The envied chance to speak the envied line.

JOHN FERGUSON (1912)

Life on the Wicked Stage

A Song from *Show Boat*

Life upon the wicked stage
Ain't ever what a girl supposes;
Stage door Johnnies aren't raging over you
With gems and roses.
When you let a feller hold your hand
(Which means an extra beer or sandwich)
Everybody whispers: 'Ain't her life a whirl?'

Though you're warned against a roué
Ruining your reputation,
When you've played around the one-night trade
Around a great big nation,
Wild old men who give you jewels and sables
Only live in Aesop's Fables.
Life upon the wicked stage is nothing for a girl! . . .

I admit it's fun to smear my face with paint
Causing everyone to think I'm what I ain't,
And I like to play a demi mondy role with soul!
Ask the hero does he like the way I lure
When I play a hussy or a paramour,
Yet once the curtain's down my life is pure
And how I dread it!

Life upon the wicked stage
Ain't ever what a girl supposes,
Stage door Johnnies aren't raging over you
With gems and roses.
If some gentleman would talk with reason
I would cancel all next season.
Life upon the wicked stage ain't nothing for a girl!

OSCAR HAMMERSTEIN 2ND (1928)

The Song of the Super

Mine's a song of tribulation,
Which I've got no sittywation,
Nothing stirring but stagnation,
And of idleness I'm sick;
Once I was a happy super,
Under Mr Harthur Cooper
(Which he'd been a galliant trooper),
Super-master at the 'Vic'.

There I oft would bear a banner
In a stern impressive manner,
For the which I got – a tanner,
Money sure, too – never tick;
Or mayhap in a procession
I perduced a good impression;
How I loved my dear perfession
When a super at the 'Vic'!

Now a noble, now a peasant,
At the right time always present,
What a life! – how bright and pleasant!
'Them was evenings, warn't they, Dick?
But them nights are gone for ever,
But no more they'll want us – never!
No more supers at the "Vic".'

Against them folks I do bear malice
Who turned it to a Coffee Pallis,
And if I ever go I shall 'iss,
As they'll find out pretty quick.
As I started, so I finish,
Though the 'ouse was often thinnish,
Nothink never won't diminish
My affection for the 'Vic'.

H J BYRON (1882)

The Boy Actor

I can remember. I can remember,
The months of November and December
Were filled for me with peculiar joys
So different from those of other boys
For other boys would be counting the days
Until end of term and holiday times
But I was acting in Christmas plays
While they were taken to pantomimes.
I didn't envy their Eton suits,
Their children's dances and Christmas trees.
My life had wonderful substitutes
For such conventional treats as these.
I didn't envy their country larks,
Their organized games in panelled halls:
While they made snow-men in stately parks
I was counting the curtain calls.

246

I remember the auditions, the nerve-racking auditions:
Darkened auditorium and empty, dusty stage,
Little girls in ballet dresses practising 'positions',
Gentlemen with pince-nez asking you your age.
Hopefulness and nervousness struggling within you,
Dreading that familiar phrase, 'Thank you dear, no more'.
Straining every muscle, every tendon, every sinew
To do your dance much better than you'd ever done before.
Think of your performance. Never mind the others,
Never mind the pianist, talent must prevail.
Never mind the baleful eyes of other children's mothers
Glaring from the corners and willing you to fail.

I can remember. I can remember.
The months of November and December
Were more significant to me
Than other months could ever be
For they were the months of high romance
When destiny waited on tip-toe,
When every boy actor stood a chance
Of getting into a Christmas show,
Not for me the dubious heaven
Of being some prefect's protégé!
Not for me the Second Eleven.
For me, two performances a day.

Ah those first rehearsals! Only very few lines:
Rushing home to mother, learning them by heart,
'Enter Left through window! – Dots to mark the cue lines:
'Exit with the others' – Still it *was* a part.
Opening performance; legs a bit unsteady,
Dedicated tension, shivers down my spine,
Powder, grease and eye-black, sticks of make-up ready
Leichner number three and number five and number nine.
World of strange enchantment, magic for a small boy
Dreaming of the future, reaching for the crown,
Rigid in the dressing-room, listening for the call-boy
'Overture Beginners – Everybody Down!'

I can remember. I can remember.
The months of November and December,
Although climatically cold and damp,
Meant more to me than Aladdin's lamp.
I see myself, having got a job,
Walking on wings along the Strand,
Uncertain whether to laugh or sob
And clutching tightly my mother's hand,
I never cared who scored the goal
Or which side won the silver cup,
I never learned to bat or bowl
But I heard the curtain going up.

NOEL COWARD (1967)

American Student Actors

We do our tensions
We do our relaxations
We do our press–ups
We do our let–downs
We do our exercises in couples
Each speaking alternately
An unpremeditated word
Accompanied by an appropriate action.
We do our thinking in as
Blurred a way as possible.
We impoverish our vocabulary
Unless it was impoverished
To start with.

Do you know
It sometimes takes us *three months*
To create
One of our improvisations?

We really do work that hard.

STEPHEN SURREY (1985)

A Student Drama Group Performs in an Old People's Home

Early evening sun leaned through the window
And warmed the carpet under their bare feet.
Powder hazed the room, and make-up sticks
Jumped nervily from clutch to clutch. Clothing
Smothered chairs, and strained plastic bags
Burst in impatience spilling properties out.

Young men aged their temples, and girls
Trenched their incipient wrinkles with thick paint.
Outside the room the corridor unrolled
Itself to life, as walking frames and sticks
Hauled slow feet to this evening's destination.
Lost, querying voices wavered and fell,

Fell into silence in the dressing-room
Where ironies oozed tangible as sweat;
The low light from the window gilded arms
Roundly lifting from flurries of lawn, to crush
Bright hair under grey acrylic wigs.
They moved in mirrors with a shocked grace.

The cast followed the same corridor down
To the same end, to the room where the audience
Waited. Full-fleshed and springing under
Their flabby mimicry, they strode in
And hurried straight to the front to be looked at,
Vital, and shadowed now under a new guilt.

And afterwards the matron said that they
All had enjoyed it, residents and staff.
'And now I have to help to bed the ones
Who can't walk back to their little flats.
Thank you again, we like these changes here.
Next week, you know, we have the acrobats.'

JOHN CASSIDY (1978)

An Actress

The part for now: kimono and Bianco,
A finish to the long day at the agency.

I couldn't live in small rooms these days:
'Spacious, second floor, deep freeze provided,
Just off Gloucester Road.' Rather garish
And 'a slum really', I read somewhere . . .
But I like it.

And visited once in three months by a father
    satisfied with a
Capable girl, he shrugs and supposes.
Can look after herself.

A Range Rover using the Residents' Parking,
A French registration. *René!*
Hi, I'll let you in! An Entryphone
Can keep out anything that threatens to be
Embarrassing.

René, have a seat, dump the books on the floor.
Oh, you're harder at twenty-six, I feel that.
Christ, a hell of a night, you can say, and then
– All over!

Yes, if life is responding I do respond.
Yes, I'm sure I respond,
There are lots of things I respond to.
I think he called himself René. (An actress
Will make any noise she considers suitable.)

– But Amanda, Christ, what a giggle, did he
Talk in French when he came?

ALAN BROWNJOHN (*c* 1973)

Walk Ons

Into another public room
With the usual dingy set
And noisy cast. The plot,
Predictable. The dialogue
Far from rich (though
Colourful). Bit Players, all.
Hags and Gravediggers. Did they get
Phone calls and availability checks?
Were contracts signed?
Enter on cue: three pretty students.
And always that
Defeated couple in the corner –
Non Speaking Artistes
With no love scenes later.

I play
Demented woman in pub,
But quietly.
Underplaying was always my style.

JULIE LUMSDEN (1989)

Mrs Worthington, Don't Put Your Daughter on the Stage

A Song

Regarding yours, dear Mrs Worthington,
Of Wednesday the 23rd,
Although your baby,
May be,
Keen on a stage career,
How can I make it clear,
That this is not a good idea.
For her to hope,

Dear Mrs Worthington,
Is on the face of it absurd.
Her personality
Is not in reality
Inviting enough,
Exciting enough
For this particular sphere.

Don't put your daughter on the stage, Mrs Worthington,
Don't put your daughter on the stage,
The profession is overcrowded
And the struggle's pretty tough
And admitting the fact
She's burning to act,
That isn't quite enough.
She has nice hands, to give the wretched girl her due,
But don't you think her bust is too
Developed for her age.
I repeat
Mrs Worthington,
Sweet
Mrs Worthington,
Don't put your daughter on the stage.

Don't put your daughter on the stage,
Mrs Worthington,
Don't put your daughter on the stage,
Though they said at the school of acting
She was lovely as Peer Gynt,
I'm afraid on the whole
An ingénue role
Would emphasize her squint.

She's a big girl, and though her teeth are fairly good
She's not the type I ever would
Be eager to engage,
No more buts,
Mrs Worthington,

NUTS,
Mrs Worthington,
Don't put your daughter on the stage.

Don't put your daughter on the stage, Mrs Worthington,
Don't put your daughter on the stage,
She's a bit of an ugly duckling
You must honestly confess,
And the width of her seat
Would surely defeat
Her chances of success,
It's a loud voice, and though it's not exactly flat,
She'll need a little more than that
To earn a living wage.
On my knees
Mrs Worthington,
Please! Mrs Worthington,
Don't put your daughter on the stage.

Don't put your daughter on the stage, Mrs Worthington,
Don't put your daughter on the stage,
One look at her bandy legs should prove
She hasn't got a chance,
In addition to which
The son of a bitch
Can neither sing nor dance,
She's a *vile* girl and uglier than mortal sin,
One look at her has put me in
A tearing bloody rage,
That sufficed,
Mrs Worthington,
Christ!
Mrs Worthington,
Don't put your daughter on the stage.

NOEL COWARD (1935)

Deep Throat

Tom
Was an Understudy
And a Gourmet –
He could TASTE success!
(So could the waiting stage –
inviting tongue
Footlights –
pearly teeth –
The red, plush darkness
An expectant
gullet).
Then
One night
Tom did
Go on . . .
And dried . . .
In dreadful silence
The jaws
Closed over
Tom.

And flushed him
out
the back passage.

Now
He teaches.

JO ANDERSON (*c* 1984)

The Actor Out of Work

the chameleon mind that aches for employment
the trained reflexes pent unused
the expressive body wasted
the attempts to re-channel creativity
the dozen hobbies listlessly pursued
the patient waiting
anticipating
the consciousness of capacity
the awareness of skill
like a greyhound held back from racing
like a tethered hawk
a locked piano
a bowless fiddle or rather a fiddle-less bow
the years of tempering and trial
the previous well-repeatable success
all that knowledge prepared to surge into action
the denial the waste the lack of function
the half-life
the quick muscles wanting to leap
the smooth voice marking time
the whole well-balanced biological instrument
ready to perform
waiting

NICHOLAS SMITH (1970)

An Old Actor

I see him in the mind's eye as he was
An actor of the old school purposely walking to the stage
   door by back streets
A book of treasured press-cuttings confirms the past
The Master Builder in Todmorden, Oedipus at Torquay –
   even a Macbeth when he was sixty
He never played in London or New York

On tour at each new town he would study the local map
So as to find a way to the theatre by the least conspicuous
    route
When I asked him why
He paused – then answered slowly
'Because, my friend, it takes away the mystery if the
    audience see you first.'

NEVILLE BRAYBROOKE (1982)

The Aged Actor Speaks

I'm having a sale of old memories.
Perhaps you'd like to buy one or two?

This one, for instance.
I know it's somewhat faded, and it has a few patches in it.
Yes, I did those myself, though I hadn't really meant to.
I'm not terribly fond of it now,
but it's certainly more serviceable than when it was new.

Here is another. Now this I really don't want to part with,
but, for reasons of health, I'm told I must.
Yes, it's in perfect condition. I've always kept it that way,
yet I've used it so often.
I can't think what I shall do without it, but I'm told I must.

And of course this one, which I suppose I ought to
share with you. It really belonged to us both. Oh, you don't
think so? But surely you remember?

I see, you just don't want your part of it.
Perhaps, then, I can let it go to someone else,
though that doesn't seem right to me.

What will you give me for the lot? Yes, all of them.
It's just that I can't bear to pick them out and dwell on
    them.
I offer them all. What do you think they're worth?

No more than that? But surely –
Yes, but don't you understand? They are my own, they are
    unique,
they're very precious.

I don't feel I could bear to part with them so cheaply.
And so, although I'm told that soon I shall have nowhere
to keep them properly, I think that, perhaps, for the time
    being
I shall hold on to them.
Yes, hold on to them, that's what I'll do.
You see, there's nothing else,
they're really all I have.

CHARLES OSBORNE (1970)

Sergei de Diaghileff (1929)

'Seroja, you're hurting. Hurt me!' Ach – I worried his arm
Against the dull class; trapped, worming, a
Wrist beneath lid. Provincial towns – Perm,
The desk-lid: grained geology of an Ernst or Dubuffet,
Neither of whom I admire. And no metaphor
Making of it a made theme. Compass-bored, elaborate
With sly graffiti. Myself bored with compasses,
Litter classified, schooling: 'Those cusps, crimped
Leaves; crisp as yeasty outside the window
They curl skyward. Say it. Say it!' – I levered him –
'Mathematics *is* unrussian!' Chinchilla.
And that was the one and only time the brigadier
Thrashed me. (Seroja broke my arm sir, he said . . .
He said) One duel I championed nature: memento.
Now strut, cultivate the strand.

'Je suis le spectre . . .' Gautier now. But what gold
Paved Peter's town! I skated, plump and suave.
Composition does not become me, since Rimsky insists.
Why not compose my friends? Mutely, imported aquarelles
Ignite the Stieglitz. That was before I invented
The avant-garde. 'Mir Isskoustva' . . . or some such aesthetic
Lab. Test-tubes to bung up Fokine, Benois
(Poor souls), I drew on my pipette and played them:
Compounded one with another to produce
That nonsense 'Armide': (effoliate the pavilion,
Tree-trunks as Louis XIV chair legs). Consider me
Neither as amateur nor dilettante. Am
The catalyst. Vatza decidedly
Lost his pants. The czarina ruffled (that was that).

The rose disrobes. I stripped the epiderm.
Never left nature her own devices (uncunning
Streams, leaves, have none). But folklorique as always
Our Russian brigades stormed the pelted,
Pelting tiers – where Astruc alternates blond with brunette.
The Châtelet repainted. No time to notice
Parisian May, I lounged in the stalls exhaustless.
'Je suis le spectre . . .' If so, Théophile, I shall haunt
Those stalls. Always to peel, to redefine,
In the light of the latest prodigy, my malaise.
With less of an idea have now than had,
What constitutes. So many prodigies have modified
Since then. Where Cocteau rhymes to define
Nijinsky dances. Oh, the dread and horror of their task!
My own abilities hinder. All theirs is mine, my
Papillons, pastiches. Wand white I have abandoned.

Now wheel me out on the verandah. Those,
Incidentally charcoals, are by – but of course you know.
Breathing! How I care more now (late my day)
For air. But not too clear and rare and precious.

This hot-house of a lagoon suits me, with
Its air fin-de-siècle and unhealthy. ' . . . de la rose
Que tu portais hier . . . ' which I carried,
Have abandoned. Carry the spectre.
Reproach my self-indulgent tears, while what's
His wife's name? Romola? – stupid, stupid

As a woman, as the droves of swans, gulls, geese,
Heckled and departed in their own brief lights
To clack in frippery: fluttering companies
Which ignore the lighthouse! Pavlova. And that
White pear, that Rubenstein! With just as much mobility
As a pear, whereas to be danced
Around she made a fine shrine. Must have
Her way and rolls about the stage – to Stravinsky
(The one man Rimsky might allow compose,
And who repaid him kindly!). Poire en lieu de grenade
Was gingered. Sugary through and *all* through
That fool Leon! As Romola: 'Jew to be sure,
But he was also something of a genius.' (Bakst).
How should *she* know (of genius)? From the day
Her 'rose' proposed she was at sea. The ninny!

' . . . que tu portais hier . . . au bal.' Spectre,
This morning shall preamble. A blue God
Incenses me in the Lido . . . Make those French windows
Taller, take away the bird! The rose's elevation
Elevates. Should seem incongruous he remind me here,
A creature essentially Russian? Not so
Incongruous to be here perhaps? Hand me those delights
Which tease my doctors – follow my finger, over where
A boy rises on his toes – those insteps – as the foam
Covers them, at the Lido's margin; leotard
For swim-suit. A Picasso. (Do you know him? Has
    designed
Several.) See him for himself, unsigned. A body by
    Nijinsky.

'Vatza, mais tu es paresseux.' Purr, purr,
'Mais viens, viens. J'ai besoin de toi.' 'Je ne peux pas
Car je suis fou.' Listen to Sergio recite his visions
'Du Baller Russe'. Vatza, Vatza
Has taught me how body is sterner,
More morally severe than mind bewitched
By lascivious environs: mimosa
Shaking its plaits over the hill's shoulder, something
In the air; immediate realisation of breathing this or that
Crisp morning; pillars emerge from mist – how body
May refuse, say look, say listen to the first,
The first ray, bird wing skip the water, the first motes
Rising serenely on their long journey to the sun. That day
In obese mirrored, guilty apartment. Moscow:
My art-junk; too many ikons, long since abandoned,
Forgot. Me naked. Him naked
And his eyes. I would have pomaded, paraded before that
    mirror,
Instead, his body's remonstrance. I parodied.
For his oblique eyes drew lids, for once revealing
Stavemarks where a Slav tune trod adagio and lightly,
To which his fear was counterpoint;
A spoiling innovation, nervously nouveau. He had

A body on him which could utter – I'm losing words. Help
Me drink . . . better. Yes, could utter at its most inactive
(Seated, say shifting slightly the weight), or most riotous
'Igor', a complete silence as of the steppe
Pacing, pacing effortlessly towards invisible pole.
He spoke with such a lump in the mouth
There must have been God in him. And the God
Was body – but not a permissive, Bacchic –
A 'but', admitting of no excesses, sighing for all the world
His nailed limbs. A question, anxious for his starved
Beasts taken for glue in the factories
Whose smoke spirals, nooses the steppe in hemp.
(And the noose closed on the dancer.)

The mirror tarnished. Room shrank from his presently
Into frowsy antiques. Routed, the array of china,
Bell-tassels, gaslit candelabra . . . Diabetic now in Venice,
The white Russian with the lacquered hair
And a taste for . . . certain tastes is, am still, abashed.
The God, my Hellenic reason, stared me
Down. Failed my slipshod, already corpulent.
I, the eloquent, darling of every spa from Dieppe to
    'Petrograd',
Say with my body, what? The neurotic flesh
Speechless than incoherent compared to his. A
Congenital vegetable! The intelligence,
Knowledge and memory in his flesh. It was Stravinsky.

Was the Urals, shawled, with no more fathers,
Husbands, sons, left to bury.
And the paradox: a Romany whore, swings bells,
Roubles, bosom, back to her surly. (Also the bull lines
Somewhere; the sad circus's attic animalry
Of that young Spaniard mentioned earlier. His
Primary blue, his Mediterranean 'as above Gourdon
That day.' His centaurs stamping
The beach). Was river, sky, pine-sweat,
But would not use these as a seasonal excuse
For poetry, the legs' laughter, clothes strewn
Over a rug . . . My cigar
Singed an overweight chair.

I dressed shabbily. Remember how his hand
Reached for, held, turned the door handle.
Then the door closed. The door
Has remained closed. It took some time to conquer
My body's shyness, his own temerity
In these matters. But the door refused, refuses
When tenement crumbles. Water!
He became confident, sly. We were several times,
How many hours, I can assure you, happy.

But I, my body, never learnt that language.
For with the first closing of a kiss something else
Should open. Darkness be broken into like a tomb.
I never hooked fingers, tugged and prised

My lazar house. Inarticulate half moan, the most
My preserved limbs managed – after intense effort –
Words as if for water, loudless, infirm, less
Free than my throat hobbles them now.
And that once I may imagine (only) remember
In Paris. Had no desire to dominate but to speak.
To speak, keep with me. (This afternoon
Rodin invites you as a faun to his conservatory).
To keep him, dominate, in some way: silence.

A death at sea? I venture to the shore,
No further; was a death certainly
Aboard ship – his departure.
How the meaningful sea has deceived me.
With Amérique du Sud, engagement, exile.
I puffed up silky: an extremely clumsy panther, dumb with
    body, rage;
Having become powerful in his world.
Now R introduces him to acupuncturists
While I weep – petulantly.

More Nijinskys, noces; more strident origins, more
Prodigious Russians. All prodigal: bitches, cocktail hours,
Balanchines. I know few dancers (and I have known many
In several ways) who could approach his mother tongue,
Which nothing trains nor breeds. Have seldom spoke
So guileless when I say, Have seen
Such speech. Any may dance, but rhetorically. Who knows
If style is what matters, especially now,
Since I turned bookish, shelving . . . ?

Venice sets as the sun raises a haze.
Glimmer of hooves, St Mark's drawn into fog.
The day raises sandy and treacherous .... That boy,
Towelled after his morning, mounts the frail,
The soon to be footed shore. Here I am,
Spectator of my last cotillon; a
Portly butterfly, sedate above the spume. Frail wings
In the mist – a perfect Balanchine? – Merde!
Water me. Ramasse mes oreillers!

ANTHONY HOWELL (1968)

Nijinski, Mad

Here sit I, Nijinski, in one corner
Of a room twelve by ten, bounded
By a nutshell which is my golden stadium
Of infinite space, and the far corner
So far, I cannot reach the far –
　　　Cannot reach –
　　　The corner.

The room is full of snow, floor to ceiling,
And I can see through it,
See right through the snow, but never reach
　　　The far corner,
Where the spotlight from the window
Never strikes, and the decent dark
Is heaped up like black sand.

If only I could reach the far corner,
I could lie naked on black sand
Away from the light where Serge
Could never see me, gold-skinned on black sand –
Lie like a fawn in the snow,
Lie in the arms of a panther who
Will protect me from Diaghilev.

And who is this with hypodermic?
Take Diaghilev away – I do not want him;
No more Diaghilev, no more,
Or the flash of the white baton ruling
The waves of music,
Or the rattle of applause beating down
Like revolver shots into the rebellious sea
As the waves shake clenched fists against
The conductor of music. All I want
Is to reach the far corner of the room
Where the black sand lies like darkness
Under the dazzling snow.

Yes, I'll bare my arm; bare arm,
Breast, hips, thighs, and be good,
Good as a little boy put to bed,
And leap no more into the limelit dangerous world,
For leap again I cannot. My bones are skeins of wool;
My muscular thighs wobble,
And there are fifty tons of trouble
On my turbanned head.

Who designed this muslin turban?
Who cut my head off? Does the panther pat it
To and fro on the black sand in the corner?
Why is the corner of the room so far, so far?

If I slide my shoulder up the shiny wall
I could begin the long journey to the far corner,
And lie there on the sand till winter melts away,
And the spring night leans over me
And dries my ridiculous tears.
So fall now, heavy eyes; fall under the snow,
    Fall and sleep.
    Fall.
    Sleep.

JONATHAN FIELD (1975)

Santa Claus

in a department store

WOLSEY, or possibly my John of Gaunt,
Was the best thing I did. Come over here,
Behind the Christmas crib. (I'm not supposed
To let the children see me having tea.)
To tell the truth I'm glad of this engagement.
Dozens applied, but all they said was Thank you,
We'll stick to Mr Borthwick.
It's nice to feel one has given satisfaction.
Time was I had it all at my finger-tips,
Could plant a whisper in the back of the pit,
Or hold them breathless with the authority
Of absolute repose – a skill despised,
Not seen, in *your* day. It amounts to this:
Technique's no more than the bare bones. There are some
Unwittingly instil the faith that Man
Is greater than he knows. This I fell short of.
        You never met my wife. You are too young.
She often came with me on tour. One night
At Nottingham, got back from the show, and there
She was. I knew at once what made her do it.
She had resented me for years. No, not
Myself, but what she knew was *in* me, my
Belief in – Sir, forgive me if I say
My 'art', for I had shown, you'll understand,
Some promise. To use her word, she felt herself
'Usurped', and by degrees, unconsciously,
She managed somehow to diminish me,
Parch all my vital streams. A look would do it.
I was a kind of shrunken river-bed
Littered with tins, old tyres, and bicycle frames.

Well, that was years ago, and by then too late
To start afresh. Yet all the while I loved her.
Explain that if you can . . . By all means, madam,
Those clocks are very popular this year.
I'll call the man in charge. No, there's no risk
Of damage. They pack the cuckoo separately.

CHRISTOPHER HASSALL (1957)

the old trouper

i ran onto mehitabel again
last evening
she is inhabiting
a decayed trunk
which lies in an alley
in greenwich village
in company with the
most villainous tom cat
i have ever seen
but there is nothing
wrong about the association
archy she told me
it is merely a plutonic
attachment
and the thing can be
believed for the tom
looks like one of pluto s demons
it is a theatre trunk
archy mehitabel told me
and tom is an old theatre cat
he has given his life
to the theatre
he claims that richard
mansfield once
kicked him out of the way
and then cried because

he had done it and
petted him
and at another time
he says in a case
of emergency
he played a bloodhound
in a production of
uncle tom s cabin
the stage is not what it
used to be tom says
he puts his front paw
on his breast and says
they don t have it any more
they don t have it here
the old troupers are gone
there s nobody can troupe
any more
they are all amateurs nowaday
they haven t got it
here
there are only
five or six of us oldtime
troupers left
this generation does not know
what stage presence is
personality is what they lack

266

personality
where would they get
the training my old friends
got in the stock companies
knew mr booth very well
ays tom
and a law should be passed
preventing anybody else
from ever playing
in any play he ever
played in
here was a trouper for you
used to sit on his knee
and purr when i was
a kitten he used to tell me
how much he valued my opinion
finish is what they lack
finish
and they haven t got it
here
and again he laid his paw
on his breast
remember mr daly very
well too
was with mr daly s company
for several years
here was art for you
here was team work
here was direction
they knew the theatre
and they all had it
here
for two years mr daly
would not ring up the curtain
unless i was in the
prompter s box
they are amateurs nowadays
rank amateurs all of them

for two seasons i played
the dog in joseph
jefferson s rip van winkle
it is true i never came
on the stage
but he knew i was just off
and it helped him
i would like to see
one of your modern
theatre cats
act a dog so well
that it would convince
a trouper like jo jefferson
but they haven t got it
nowadays
they haven t got it
here
jo jefferson had it he had it
here
i come of a long line
of theatre cats
my grandfather
was with forrest
he had it he was a real trouper
my grandfather said
he had a voice
that used to shake
the ferryboats
on the north river
once he lost his beard
and my grandfather
dropped from the
fly gallery and landed
under his chin
and played his beard
for the rest of the act
you don t see any theatre
cats that could do that

nowadays
they haven t got it they
haven t got it
here
once i played the owl
in modjeska s production
of macbeth
i sat above the castle gate
in the murder scene
and made my yellow
eyes shine through the dusk

like an owl s eyes
modjeska was a real
trouper she knew how to pick
her support i would like
to see any of these modern
theatres cats play the owl s eyes
to modjeska s lady macbeth
but they haven t got it nowadays
they haven t got it
here

mehitabel he says
both our professions
are being ruined
by amateurs
                    archy

DON MARQUIS (1927)

He the player under Irving
He the mighty man of grease paint
And the teller of great stories
Of the tribes that were real actors
When the theatre was the theatre.

DONALD WOLFIT (1943)

He's a Pro

A Song

I thought it was great when I went on the stage
About six-and-a-half months ago;
'Cos everybody was so kind to me
When they found out that I was a 'Pro';
But a fire broke out in my lodgings one night
And the fire-men were there instantly,
They saved everybody right down to the cat
But they never once tried to save me.
I dashed to the window and heard with dismay
A big fire brigade Captain to somebody say:

    'He's a Pro! He's a Pro!
    And he'll make us all laugh in a minute or so.'
    I could feel myself cooking, my shirt was alight,
    So I stood on the window–sill trembling with fright;
    The fire-men were laughing at me
    And I heard someone say down below,
    'Let him do us a turn 'cos I don't think he'll burn,
    He's a Pro! He's a Pro!'

I had a new song I was trying to learn
So I picked out a quiet place to go;
I hired a small boat and went out on the sea
And I started to study you know;
I was learning the words and the melody fine
When the bloke who was rowing me said
'Do you like a big hit?' I said 'Yes' so he hit me
And knocked the words out of me head.
I fell in the water, a shark came my way,
But it wouldn't touch me 'cos it heard a cod say:

'He's a Pro! He's a Pro!'
I'd been swimming around for an hour or so
Then a ship came in sight and the captain cried 'Jim!
There's a man overboard, throw the lifeline to him.'
Jim came and peeped over the side
And when he saw me down there below,
To the captain he ran. He said 'That's not a man,
He's a Pro! He's a Pro!'

I one time appeared in a swell Music Hall
Where I thought I should make such a hit;
The band played my music, I ran on the stage,
But a battle was on in the Pit;
Well I started to sing 'All that I ask is Love,'
I remember no more after that.
All that I asked was 'Love' but the boys up above
Gave me something more solid than that.
I woke up in hospital the following day,
And I just recollect hearing somebody say:

'He's a Pro! He's a Pro!'
'And the poor devil looks like one too!' said Nurse Flo.
Then the doctor said 'Nurse, there's but one thing to do,
We must operate on him to pull him right through.'
He said 'Now do you think he'd hurt
If we starved him for twelve hours or so?'
The Nurse said 'Have no fears, he's been starving for
    years,
He's a Pro! He's a Pro!'

MAGINI (1921)

Epitaph for an Actor in the Television Age

When they laid him on his final bed,
'He made a mess of his life,' they said;
'His money went on fun and drink –
'Will anyone mourn him much, do you think?
'He never fought for any cause,
'Or added to our stock of laws.
'He nothing said of peace or war –
'A useless life we must deplore.'

And somewhere, where we cannot look,
A hand wrote all this in a book.
Then added one more paragraph
About how he made millions laugh.
And, sometimes, some of them exclaim:
'I used to like old whatsisname.'

NICHOLAS SMITH (1980)

Why Do We Do It?

The last light goes out,
And The Space is left in silence.
The Watchers have slipped back into their own world.
Dust falls on Velvet.

Why do we remain, then?
What promise binds us to this art?
We never truly leave The Space
Nor hope to fill it.
Perhaps it is inside us from our birth.

The shadows we created
Draw us further from the Real,
'Til Life becomes a makebelieve
And Magic is Reality.

The last light goes out,
And echoes slowly drift
Through empty air.

But deep within that emptiness
Something –
Some thing,
Remains
And always draws us back again.

ANNA THOMAS (1989)

'Benefit for the Theatrical Fund'

From the Prologue spoken by
Garrick at his last performance

A vet'ran see, whose last act on the stage
Intreats your smiles for sickness and for age,
Their cause I plead, plead it with heart and mind;
A fellow feeling makes one wond'rous kind.

DAVID GARRICK (1776)

THE WORLD A STAGE

Whence are we, and why are we? Of what scene
The actors or spectators?

PERCY BYSSHE SHELLEY (1821)

Prologue

My life is like a music-hall,
Where, in the impotence of rage,
Chained by enchantment to my stall,
I see myself upon the stage
Dance to amuse a music-hall.

'Tis I that smoke this cigarette,
Lounge here, and laugh for vacancy,
And watch the dancers turn; and yet
It is my very self I see
Across the cloudy cigarette.

My very self that turns and trips,
Painted, pathetically gay,
An empty song upon the lips
In make-believe of holiday:
I, I, this thing that turns and trips!

The light flares in the music-hall,
The light, the sound, that weary us;
Hour follows hour, I count them all,
Lagging, and loud, and riotous:
My life is like a music-hall.

ARTHUR SYMONS (1897)

All our pride is but a jest;
None are worst and none are best;
Grief and joy, and hope and fear
Play the pageants everywhere:
Vain opinion all doth sway,
And the world is but a play.

THOMAS CAMPION (1601)

275

The World's A Stage

1

The world's a stage. The light is in one's eyes.
The Auditorium is extremely dark.
The more dishonest get the larger rise;
The more offensive make the greater mark.
The women on it prosper by their shape,
Some few by their vivacity. The men,
By tailoring in breeches and in cape.
The world's a stage – I say it once again.

The scenery is very much the best
Of what the wretched drama has to show,
Also the prompter happens to be dumb.
We drink behind the scenes and pass a jest
On all our folly; then, before we go
Loud cries for 'Author' . . . but he doesn't come.

2

The world's a stage – and I'm the Super man,
And no one seems responsible for salary.
I roar my part as loudly as I can
And all I mouth I mouth it to the gallery.
I haven't got another rhyme in 'alery';
It would have made a better job, no doubt,
If I had left attempt at Rhyming out,
Like Alfred Tennyson adapting Malory.

The world's a stage, the company of which
Has very little talent and less reading:
But many a waddling heathen painted bitch
And many a standing cad of gutter breeding.
    We sweat to learn our book: for all our pains
    We pass. The Chucker-out alone remains.

3

The world's a stage. The trifling entrance fee
Is paid (by proxy) to the registrar.
The Orchestra is very loud and free
But plays no music in particular.
They do not print a programme, that I know.
The cast is large. There isn't any plot.
The acting of the piece is far below
The very worst of modernistic rot.

The only part about it I enjoy
Is what was called in English the Foyay.
There will I stand apart awhile and toy
With thought, and set my cigarette alight;
And then – without returning to the play –
On with my coat and out into the night.

HILAIRE BELLOC (1923)

All the World's A Stage

From *As You Like It*, Act Two, Scene VII

All the world's a stage,
And all the men and women merely players;
They have their exits and their entrances;
And one man in his time plays many parts,
His acts being seven ages. At first the infant,
Mewling and puking in the nurse's arms;
Then the whining school-boy, with his satchel
And shining morning face, creeping like snail
Unwillingly to school. And then the lover,
Sighing like furnace, with a woeful ballad
Made to his mistress' eyebrow. Then a soldier,
Full of strange oaths, and bearded like the pard,
Jealous in honour, sudden and quick in quarrel,

Seeking the bubble reputation
Even in the cannon's mouth. And then the justice,
In fair round belly with good capon lin'd,
With eyes severe and beard of formal cut,
Full of wise saws and modern instances;
And so he plays his part. The sixth age shifts
Into the lean and slipper'd pantaloon,
With spectacles on nose and pouch on side,
His youthful hose, well sav'd, a world too wide
For his shrunk shank; and his big manly voice,
Turning again toward childish treble, pipes
And whistles in his sound. Last scene of all,
That ends this strange eventful history,
Is second childishness and mere oblivion;
Sans teeth, sans eyes, sans taste, sans everything.

WILLIAM SHAKESPEARE (c 1600)

To the Memory of Mr W Shakespeare
Prefaced to the First Folio of Shakespeare's works

We wondered, Shakespeare, that thou went'st so soon
From the world's stage to the grave's tiring-room.
We thought thee dead, but this thy printed worth,
Tells thy spectators that thou went'st but forth
To enter with applause. An actor's art,
Can die, and live, to act a second part.
That's but an exit of mortality;
This, a re-entrance to a plaudite.

ANON (1623)

Drama in the Heart

Drama's vitalest expression
    Is the Common Day
That arises, sets about us;
    Other tragedy
Perish in the recitation,
    This the more exert
When the audience is scattered
    And the boxes shut.

Hamlet to himself were Hamlet
    Had not Shakespeare wrote,
Though the Romeo leave no record
    Of his Juliet,
It were tenderer enacted
    In the human heart –
Only theatre recorded
    Owner cannot shut.

EMILY DICKINSON (1863)

Life's little stage is a small eminence,
Inch-high the grave above.

EDWARD YOUNG (1747)

The Author to his Book

From *An Apology for Actors*

The world's a theatre, the earth a stage
Which God and nature doth with actors fill,
Kings have their entrance in due equipage,
And some their parts play well and others ill.

The best no better are (in this theatre)
Where every humour's fitted in his kind;
This a true subject acts, and that a traitor,
The first applauded, and the last confin'd;
This plays an honest man, and that a knave,
A gentle person this, and he a clown,
One man is ragged, and another brave;
All men have parts, and each man acts his own.
She a chaste lady acteth all her life,
A wanton courtesan another plays.
This, covets marriage love, that, nuptial strife,
Both in continual action spend their days.
Some citizens, some soldiers, born to adventure,
Shepherds and sea-men; then our play's begun,
When we are born, and to the world first enter,
And all find exits when their parts are done.
If then the world a theatre present,
As by the roundness it appears most fit,
Built with star-galleries of high ascent,
In which Jehove doth as spectator sit,
And chief determiner to applaud the best,
And their endeavours crown with more than merit,
But by their evil actions dooms the rest,
To end disgrac'd whilst others praise inherit,
   He that denies then theatres should be,
   He may as well deny a world to me.

THOMAS HEYWOOD (1612)

My soul, sit thou a patient looker-on;
Judge not the play before the play is done.
Her plot hath many changes; every day
Speaks a new scene; the last act crowns the play.

FRANCIS QUARLES (1635)

Plays

Alas, how soon the hours are over,
Counted us out to play the lover!
And how much narrower is the stage,
Allotted us to play the sage!

But when we play the fool, how wide
The theatre expands! Beside,
How long the audience sits before us!
How many prompters! What a chorus!

WALTER SAVAGE LANDOR (1846)

On the Everyday Theatre

Actors
You who perform plays in great houses
Under false suns and before silent faces
Look sometimes at
The theatre whose stage is the street.
The everyday theatre
Common, unrewarded with honour,
But of this earth, living,
Made from the traffic of men together.
The theatre whose stage is the street.
Here the woman from next door –
Gives us the landlord.
Imitating his stream of words,
How well she shows him up
Trying to keep the conversation off
The burst water pipe.
Young men mime to giggling girls
In parks at dusk
How girls resist yet while resisting
Beckon to them with their breasts.

And there the drunk
Playing the pulpit parson
Refers the less fortunate among us
To the golden fields of paradise.
Earnest and gay the theatre of the street
Has uses
And dignity
Not like parrot or ape
Do these men imitate for imitation's sake,
Unconcerned with what they show
Save that they themselves are imitating well.
They have their purposes in mind.
And in this, great actors that you are,
Masters of imitation,
Do not ever lag behind.
However polished your art
Do not step too far
From the everyday theatre,
The theatre whose stage is the street.
Look – the man at the corner re-enacting
The accident
Thus he gives the driver at his wheel
To the crowd for trial.
Thus the victim, who seems old.
Of each he only gives so much
That the accident be understood
Yet each lives before your eyes
And each he presents in a manner
To suggest the accident avoidable.
So the event is understood
And yet can still astound:
The moves of both could have been different.
Now he shows how both could have moved
To circumvent the accident.
This witness is free from superstition.
Never to the stars
Does he abandon his mortals
But only to their own mistakes.

Notice too
How serious and careful his imitation.
He knows that much depends on his precision:
Whether the innocent is ruined,
Whether the injured one receives his compensation.
See him now do what he has already done
Over again.
He hesitates,
Calls on his memory's aid,
Doubts if his imitation is truly good,
Stops to demand correction for this detail or that.
Observe with reverence.
And observe with astonishment:
This imitator never loses himself in his imitation.
Never does he lend himself whole
To the person he plays.
He remains, disengaged, the one who shows.
The man he represents has not confided in him.
Nor does he share
The feelings or views of this man.
He knows but little of him.
His imitation does not engender
A third
Composed in roughly equal parts
Of him and the other,
A third in whom but one heart beats
And one brain thinks.
His senses collected he, the performer,
Stands and gives us
The man next door,
A stranger.
In your theatres
You would take us in
With your magical transformation
Somewhere between
Dressing room and stage:
An actor leaves his room
A king enters the play.

And at this I've seen the stage hands
Laugh out loud with their bottles of beer.
Our performer there on the corner
Spins no such spell.
He's no sleep-walker you may not address,
Nor high priest at service.
Interrupt as you will.
Calmly he will reply
And when you have had your say
Continue his performance.
Don't declare this man is not an artist.
By creating this distinction between the world and
　　yourselves
You banish yourselves from the world.
If you declare:
He is no artist,
He may reply:
You are not men.
A worse reproach by far.
Declare instead:
He is an artist because a man.
What he does we may do
With more perfection
Thus gaining honour.
Yet we practise
What is universal,
Human,
To be seen every hour in the teeming streets,
Almost as popular as eating and breathing.

Thus all your acting
Leads back to daily life.
Our masks, you should say,
Are nothing special
If they remain mere masks.
Over there the seller of scarves
Dons the master's hat
Dangles a cane

Pastes on a lady-killing moustache
And behind his stall
Cake-walks up and down
To prove how hat, moustache and scarf
Indeed change men
Most favourably.
They, like us, you should say,
Have their verses.
The newspaper sellers cry their headlines
With a rhythm to heighten
Effect and make their own refrains
Easier to sustain.
We learn, you should say,
The words of others
But likewise too salesmen and lovers learn.
And how often
The sayings of people
Are repeated.
Thus common the quotation, the verse and the mask
Yet uncommon a mask seen large
Uncommon a beautifully said verse
And uncommon the intelligent quotation.

But let us understand each other.
You may perform better than he
Whose stage is the street.
Still your achievement will be less
If your theatre is less
Meaningful than his,
If it touches less
Deeply the lives of those who watch,
If its reasons
Are less,
Or its usefulness.

BERTOLT BRECHT (c 1930)
(Trans. Edith Anderson)

Theatre

Oh look, a dog walking along by himself!
I can tell he wants me to believe he has
A destination.

When I dragged the curtains aside, they became
A fourth wall enclosing his performance of
A purpose, strolling

Across the stage of the street not swiftly, not
Diverted by anything. And see, a cat
Which connives at this

Dog's desire to seem busy, therefore just sits
And knows he will be safe. What fine perception!
The dog exits, left.

And he is now in the past, the cat and I
Have entered the present where nothing happens.
And three large blue cars

Driving past is not dramatic, only part
Of everyday life. Except that in that house
A curtain opens,

And a face cranes out with crude astonishment
At three glossy cars! They cross his empty stage,
They want him to think

They had a destination and a purpose,
And at the corner a policeman has connived
At their busy wish.

We might try hard, but this other face and I
Cannot see the same production. Entranced, he
Stands there gazing, but

For me events of tables and chairs inside
The room behind me are more amazing now.
Let the play go on

In the eye of this other beholder, I
Shall finish with it and pull my curtains, sad
At so many walls.

ALAN BROWNJOHN (1987)

'This Wild Drama'

Life's a long tragedy; this globe the stage,
Well fix'd and well adorn'd with strong machines,
Gay fields, and skies, and seas; the actors many:
The plot immense.

ISAAC WATTS (1705)

Act first, this Earth, a stage so gloom'd with woe
    You all but sicken at the shifting scenes.
And yet be patient. Our Playwright may show
    In some fifth act what this wild Drama means.

ALFRED, LORD TENNYSON (1889)

Young Master's Account of a Puppet Show

What wondrous pretty things I've seen,
    How were my eyes delighted!
Fine lords and ladies, King and Queen,
    With gold and silver dighted.

The little creatures, how they spoke
   With voices shrill and squeaking!
Methinks I see their puny look,
   And still I hear them speaking.

Here's one in love o'er head and ears,
   Tries every way to move her;
While with a scorn the lady hears
   Her sighing, dying lover.

The wretch, despairing to obtain
   Her favour or her graces,
With sword or halter ends his pain,
   And kinder death embraces.

The lady, when she's told his fate,
   Distracted with her passion,
Curses her scorn, alas! too late,
   And dies with mere vexation.

Next Punch, a bragging rogue, appears,
   With huge and strutting belly;
Talks big and swaggers, huffs and stares,
   And who but he, he'll tell you.

To show his valour, takes a switch,
   And trims poor Cherry's jacket;
She cries and scolds; he kicks her breech,
   And vows the jade does lack it.

His wit and jokes, and jibing jeers,
   Made all who heard him merry;
Yet I could lug him by the ears
   For beating honest Cherry.

And then the puppets, how they danc'd
   All sweetly to the fiddle,
Till blust'ring Punch along advanc'd
   And jumped into the middle.

He puts 'em out and throws 'em down,
   And then, the more to charm ye,
Kicks 'em about, and swaggers round,
   As if he'd slain an army.

Such the diversion, such the sport
   The little mimics gave us,
So brisk, so lively, so alert,
   As if they would out-brave us.

When I this pigmy troop survey'd,
   And all their various actions,
Thus to myself I softly said,
   And these were my reflections:

Daily we see such things are done
   As these small folks exhibit,
A lover's sighs, a lady's frown,
   And rogues upon a gibbet.

Another there to power grown
   Just like to Punchenello
Bounces and cracks of what he's done
   And is a mighty fellow.

Fiercely he looks, and talks as big,
   And blusters like a Hector,
On poorer folks he runs his rig,
   And huffs like Lord Protector

But try his courage, soon you'll find
　That, though he roared and bullied,
Patient, he'll take a kick behind,
　Nor think his honour sullied.

Many such heroes may be seen
　In this great world about us;
And Punch's little mimic scene
　Does with our own but flout us.

JOHN MARCHANT (1731)

Upper Circle Incident

The man collapsed behind me
just before the curtain,
I, with a Doctor, tended him
as he lay prone. Uncertain

as what to do, I called an usher
where the patrons mingle,
minutes passed, then help arrived,
I heard its urgent jingle.

Meantime, his body quivered
among the seated throng,
the lady GP then announced
that he had bit his tongue.

He rallied for a moment,
and asked us where he was,
she told him in a clear voice;
no matter – for his stars

last night were set against him,
and he was never destined
to stay and hear Fidelio,
for then the white van hastened

and placed its sickly passenger
in better hands, albeit a
different sort of building,
a different kind of theatre.

MONICA HOYER (1988)

To the Audience

You sit and watch the stage
Your back is turned –
To what?

The firing squad
Shoots in the back of the neck
Whole nations have been caught
Looking the wrong way

I want to remind you
Of what you forgot to see
On the way here
To listen to what
You were too busy to hear
To ask you to believe
What you were too ashamed to admit

If what you see on the stage displeases
You run away
Lucky audience!
Is there no innocence in chains
In the world you run to?
No child starving
Because your world's too weak
And all the rich too poor
To feed it?

On the stage actors talk of life and imitate death
You must solve their problems in your life
I remind you
They show future deaths

EDWARD BOND (1971)

Hiss the Villain

If we spotted Polonius on the station platform,
We would dodge into the waiting room.
If Hedda bore down upon us in the High Street,
Suffocating in fur and affectation,
We would remember something forgotten in the grocer's.
Falstaff, drunk, lecherous and burping,
And Doolittle the Twister, would be our unwelcome
    guests.
Yet we take delight in their company in the playhouse.
For though it is the church which bids us
Love our enemies, it is the playhouse
Which enables us to do it.
It is only in life that we hiss the villain now.

JONATHAN FIELD (1971)

'Guilty Creatures'

From *Hamlet*, Act Two, Scene II

. . . I have heard
That guilty creatures, sitting at a play,
Have by the very cunning of the scene
Been struck so to the soul that presently
They have proclaim'd their malefactions;

For murder, though it have no tongue, will speak
With most miraculous organ. I'll have these players
Play something like the murder of my father
Before mine uncle. I'll observe his looks;
I'll tent him to the quick. If 'a do blench,
I know my course. The spirit that I have seen
May be a devil; and the devil hath power
T' assume a pleasing shape; yea, and perhaps
Out of my weakness and my melancholy,
As he is very potent with such spirits,
Abuses me to damn me. I'll have grounds
More relative than this. The play's the thing
Wherein I'll catch the conscience of the King.

WILLIAM SHAKESPEARE (*c* 1600)

The Play's the Thing

This play is not the truth: it is a play.
My daughter watches it, and tells me so.
It is a play. In 1633
Someone invented it, and wrote it down.
Now, in the present, we sit down and watch
This playing truth, or truthful play, and say
It is not true. Such words, such blood, are not
True to our knowledge, or our sense of what
We know as truth.
                    And then we go to bed,
Disturbed by untruth, or by what was said
Closely enough to truth to make us lie
Awake in troubledness, and then to drown
In dreams where no door opens, every latch
Locks at our hand, and all things falsify.

ANTHONY THWAITE (1982)

Actor Rehearsing

Lo! Thy dread empire, chaos! is restored:
Light dies before thy uncreating word:
Thy hand, great anarch! lets the curtain fall,
And universal darkness buries all.

ALEXANDER POPE, *The Dunciad*

I

Prologue

A bed, a chair, a table, and a cupboard,
Stand in this bare room and rattle at my tread:
Save for these and a mirror is my room quite bare:
It is empty like a honeycomb that holds no honey
For the sun never comes to load my cell with light.
The paper that strips itself from off my walls
Is canvas dropped away and rotting from its scaffolding:
My moonlight tempered with black smoke –
The magnesium lights that groan before each flare.
It is too dark for reflections to play upon the walls
So I have no gilded lattices against my bruised plaster:
My window-panes like broken mirrors
Showing me no starlight, that wood of golden trees –
I'm left with nothing but bare boards and rain-soaked
    ceiling:
The creaking furniture my altar,
And this mirror, broken and misty like my past,
Which I still might look in, could I gather its spent light
Splintered in little pools upon the floor.

The magnesium lights that have no steady flame,
That cannot hover like a star on wings of light,
Poised, with spread feathers that they dip from time to time
In the gold-lit water that their passage leaves,
But groan before each flare
Catching their breath because the wind blows strong
Coming at us every way it can

Through cracked windows and between the shafts of
   scaffolding,
Using what is old and done and what is not yet finished,
Burn less and less;
I wait long moments in the wings until they're ready
As though I stood and waited for their dying words,
Scarce whispered,
And when this puff of strength comes
I walk to the stage front,
Living in this radiance while its life-beat lasts.
Here am I bathing in this silver water
Speaking with my action while I mouth the words out loud
And move with my metaphors,
Like the salamander while my light lasts
I live in the fire's heart, lit air, or shadowed water.
Just when I've started, when I'm finished like a statue,
Carved and coloured, comprehensible to all,
Living in one moment the whole span of life
Where ten failing years weep no longer than a creaking door
And before the hinge is silent time is mute and sad once
   more,
The light dies out:
It wheezes and gasps for breath before night stifles it,
Crumbling to white powder that fills and stains the air,
It dies and leaves my eyes dazed,
Smarting with this powder,
While parhelions, those mocking lights, play in the wind –
False mirrors for my acting that my tired eyes project for
   me.
I make for this starlight and its golden leaves of light,
But they sway too high above my head to help me
And before I can reach to them they flicker and fade out:
I stagger in the darkness turned mute as well as blind,
While the parhelions at some other point of wind,
Fostered by its softness, blow their fires alight once more;
I am left alone in the darkness, stone statue in chill water,
I am alone in my bare room again,
Hungry and cold.

Here will I stay a little: I'll lie upon my bed
And look for vision, like the painter, on damp plaster,
Making my own images from the mouldering marks of
   damp;
Or I'll listen to the wind's cheap flute that sets my window
   dancing –
I'll lie awake and hearken to the barking dogs;
I shall not sleep at all. . . .

II

At his Mirror

'Have I time yet? Has the bell rung?
For I cannot act great Caesar with my cloak half-hung.
Hold the lantern higher so it lights my head.'
The corridors are draughty and as long as a railway,
Icy to tread along, and tiring as a stairway;
Nothing fits; no doors or windows close.

He looks into his mirror and the glass makes him dramatic:
Like the eagle if it answered to the hunter's horn
Screeching through thin air this echo came forlorn:
Like the eagle's voice this echo out of the mirror to his
   aching self,
For it shows him as he'd have himself before the light,
All else subordinate, the whole world hushed:
Each knoll a cliff, and every tree a brimming cove
Where warriors in blue water wade
As they strike through leaves like the tide upon the sand
And the branches sway and sing like the sighing strand,
While they break out of this green world,
From one mirror to another.
Here shepherds tune their madrigals,
Where rivers, by the sun loosed, run down in waterfalls
Of shaking fleeces, white as wool,
And tune them to its falling, swift and cool
As it rises past those dolphin-backs the sunken rocks.
Next he holds himself before this echo

Like a man at a cave's mouth, bold and loud,
Who shouts into its depths and gets his answer back,
Fierce and brazen does he show out of the mirror,
He sees himself in armour, plumed and plated,
Unhelmeted, his thin hair blown back
Like the flag behind its flagstaff in the high,
Shrill wind of his triumph:
He is high up, rolled in glory
Smooth as water moving in its river-bed
Over hot rocks and treacherous shoals of sand:
There is nothing hostile, no wind to drown his trumpets.
He can choose his personalities and move among them,
Constantly changing,
Like the hare who doubles on his tracks to hide them:
Or keep to one character
Like a dynasty who rules a country,
Playing the same politics whoever guides the play:
He can hold both reins and have the power to choose
    between them,
Fit into the circumstance, or make his own conditions,
Act in his own character, or wear a cloak that's made for him,
For it blows cold in these corridors.
These set scenes built in stone
With porticos that open like the trumpet's mouth
Carrying his voice along for wind to run with it
Out from these pillars till it hangs upon the air
Hiding with its brazen wings all other voices quivering
    there,
That it mutes with these stiff feathers so their tongues
    cannot be heard: . . .

IV

Performance

The lights are so low that I cannot see to stumble:
I dare not move, but have to stand,
Stone still,
Like a statue in chill water:

I will go through all my tragedies;
Though no one answers me:
Such is my method: with every character left open
I work by myself, till an echo from steep battlements
Treads down to meet me with iron feet and beaked eagle voice
Challenging my tragedies.
It is for this I stand here
Speaking in this dark night;
Since starlight – that wood of gold trees at our windows –
That hedge that lies between us – the lit fronds of the
    footlights –
So dimly burn, and have such chattering warmth
To light us.
This poor heat is our only hope,
This light our only help from heaven,
And that but a travesty,
A sunlight through many mirrors shown.
There is no safety for us,
But what we store ourselves
Against strong tides and fevers:
Put up no more statues, then, but pray for virtue,
For wells of sweet water in this parched, dry sand.
I can show you many characters,
Many moulds to take your metal,
Many voices, pipes, and organ notes,
Much music to unravel:
I can strike with the silver key,
But you must tune your notes.

Answer me, answer me, before I drown,
My steely, tragic armour will bear me down:
It is dark, darker still, almost night:
I die in these direful words; I lose my sight:
'Lo! thy dread empire, Chaos! is restored:
Light dies before thy uncreating word:
Thy hand, great anarch, lets the curtain fall,
And universal darkness buries all.'

SACHEVERELL SITWELL (1924)

They All Want to Play Hamlet

hey all want to play Hamlet.
hey have not exactly seen their fathers killed
or their mothers in a frame-up to kill,
or an Ophelia dying with a dust gagging the heart,
ot exactly the spinning circles of singing golden spiders,
ot exactly this have they got at nor the meaning of flowers –
  O flowers, flowers slung by a dancing girl – in the saddest
  play the inkfish, Shakespeare, ever wrote;
et they all want to play Hamlet because it is sad like all actors
  are sad and to stand by an open grave with a joker's skull in
  the hand and then to say over slow and say over slow wise,
  keen, beautiful words masking a heart that's breaking, breaking,
his is something that calls and calls to their blood.
hey are acting when they talk about it and they know it is acting
  to be particular about it and yet: They all want to play Hamlet.

CARL SANDBURG (1920)

Understudy

She's a trained low-profile lady
obeying the signs –
Keep out, Keep off the grass –
keeping her place backstage
until her call
from the undressing-room. All
her performances submerged
in her major-minor role
of understudy.

PHOEBE HESKETH (1989)

Life's but a walking shadow, a poor player,
That struts and frets his hour upon the stage,
And then is heard no more.

WILLIAM SHAKESPEARE (1606)

299

Exit

Could I but choose my exit, I would say: –
'Now we approach the evening of the play,
The curtain has gone up upon Act Three
And now the plot has ceased to interest me.
There was a tale but it is almost told,
So let me go before I grow too old,
Before I miss my lines and shame my part,
Before I desecrate my much loved art,
While I can hear the call bell when it rings
And I can still walk upright to the wings.'

NONIE W S CHRISTIAN (*c* 1988)

On the Life of Man

What is our life? A play of passion,
Our mirth the music of division,
Our mothers' wombs the tiring houses be,
Where we are dressed for this short comedy,
Heaven the judicious sharp spectator is,
That sits and marks who still doth act amiss,
Our graves that hide us from the searching sun,
Are like drawn curtains when the play is done,
Thus march we playing to our latest rest,
Only we die in earnest, that's no jest.

SIR WALTER RALEGH (1612)

When we are born, we cry that we are come
To this great stage of fools.

WILLIAM SHAKESPEARE (1605)

'This Insubstantial Pageant'
From *The Tempest*, Act Four, Scene I

Our revels now are ended. These our actors,
As I foretold you, were all spirits, and
Are melted into air, into thin air;
And, like the baseless fabric of this vision,
The cloud-capp'd towers, the gorgeous palaces,
The solemn temples, the great globe itself,
Yea, all which it inherit, shall dissolve,
And, like this insubstantial pageant faded,
Leave not a rack behind. We are such stuff
As dreams are made on; and our little life
Is rounded with a sleep.

WILLIAM SHAKESPEARE (*c* 1613)

Acknowledgements

The editor wishes to thank the staff of libraries used in the compilation of this anthology, in particular the British Library, the Poetry Library and the Library of the University of East Anglia.

For permission to reproduce poems in the collection, acknowledgement is made to the following:

For Fleur Adcock's 'Shakespeare's Hotspur', © Fleur Adcock 1983, from Fleur Adcock's *Selected Poems* (1983), to Oxford University Press; for Conrad Aiken's 'Curtain' from *Collected Poems* by Conrad Aiken, copyright © 1953, 1981 by Conrad Aiken, to Oxford University Press, Inc; for Jo Anderson's 'Deep Throat', to the author; for Marie Anthony's 'In Pursuit of a Bear' and 'The Actor', to the author; for Leo Aylen's 'Old Age Make-up', published in *Jumping Shoes*, Sidgwick and Jackson (1983), to the author; for Hilaire Belloc's 'The World's a Stage' from *The Complete Verse of Hilaire Belloc*, Pimlico (Random Century) (1991), to the Peters Fraser and Dunlop Group Ltd; for Guy Boas's 'The Audience', 'Chocolates', 'The Critic' and 'The Repertory Actor', to Punch; for Edward Bond's 'To the Audience', © 1978 Edward Bond, from *Theatre Poems and Songs* (1978), to Methuen London; for Neville Braybrooke's 'An Old Actor', first published in *New Poetry*, edited by John Fuller, Hutchinson (1982), to the author; for Bertolt Brecht's 'On Judging' and 'On the Everyday Theatre' (translated by Edith Anderson) and 'The Curtains', 'The Portrayal of Past and Present in One' and 'The Lighting' (translated by John Willett) from *Bertolt Brecht: Poems 1913–1956*, Methuen London (1987), to the author's estate, translators and publishers; for Alan Brownjohn's 'An Actress' and 'Theatre' from *Collected Poems of Alan Brownjohn*, Hutchinson (1988), to the author and publishers; for John Cassidy's 'A Student Drama Group Performs in an Old People's Home' from *Night Cries* by John Cassidy, Bloodaxe Books (1982), PBS Recommendation, to the author; for Charles Causley's 'Laurence Olivier's Richard III' from *Farewell Angie Weston* by Charles Causley, Hand and Flower Press (1951), to the author and publishers; for Nonie W S Christian's 'Exit', to Mrs Hazel Lunt; for Noel Coward's 'Mrs Worthington' from *Noel Coward: The Lyrics*, Methuen London (1965), to the Noel Coward Estate and the publishers; and for 'The Boy Actor' and 'Social Grace' from *Not Yet the Dodo*, Heinemann (1967), to the Noel Coward Estate; for Cyril Cusack's 'Number One' from *Between the Acts and Other Poems*, Colin Smythe (1990), to the author and publisher; for Alan Dunnett's 'In Bed with Macbeth' from *In the Savage Gap* (1989) and 'The Extra' from *Hurt Under Your Arm*, Envoi Poets (1991), to the author; for Tom Durham's 'Alpha Beta', to the author; for T S Eliot's 'Gus: The Theatre Cat' from *Old Possum's Book of Practical Cats* (1939) by T S Eliot, to Faber and Faber Ltd; for D J Enright's 'All's Well that Ends' from *Poetry for Shakespeare 2*, Globe Playhouse Trust (1973), to the author, publisher, and Watson and Little Ltd; for U A Fanthorpe's 'Robert Lindsay's Hamlet' from *Voices Off*, Peterloo Poets (1984), to the author and publishers; for Herbert Farjeon's 'Charge of the Late Brigade' from *Spread It Abroad*, The Saville Theatre (1936), and 'On Actors' from *The Herbert Farjeon Omnibus*, Hutchinson (1942), to the author's estate and the publishers; for Michael Foley's 'Sacred Fire' and 'Under the Stage', to the author; for Les Freeman's 'A Theatre Dies: Stockton Empire', to Peter Durkin; for Robert Graves's 'Act V, Scene 5' from *Ten Poems More*, Hours Press, Paris (1930) and 'A Visit to Stratford' from *Robert Graves:*

ACKNOWLEDGEMENTS

Poems (1914–26), Heinemann (1927), to A P Watt Ltd on behalf of the Trustees of the Robert Graves Copyright Trust; for Stephen Haggard's 'To Peggy Ashcroft' from *I'll Go to Bed at Noon*, Faber and Faber (1944), to the author's estate and the publishers; for Oscar Hammerstein 2nd's 'Life on the Wicked Stage' from *Show Boat*, Chappell (1928), to Polygram Music Publications Ltd; for Christopher Hassall's 'Santa Claus in a Department Store' from *The Red Leaf: Poems* by Christopher Hassall, Oxford University Press (1957), to the author's estate and the publishers; for Henri's 'To Miss Nelson on her Visit to Wells', to the Trustees of the National Maritime Museum; for A P Herbert's 'Song of the Stage Hands' from *Full Enjoyment and Other Verses*, Methuen (1952), 'When Crummles Played' from *When Crummles Played*, Lyric Theatre, Hammersmith (1927), and 'This Is a Theatre', to A P Watt on behalf of Crystal Hale and Jocelyn Herbert; for Phoebe Hesketh's 'Understudy' from *Collected Poems*, Enitharmon Press (1989), to the author; for Anthony Howell's 'Sergei de Diaghileff (1929)', Turret Books (1968), to the author; for Monica Hoyer's 'Upper Circle Incident', to the author; for Aldous Huxley's 'Theatre of Varieties' from *The Collected Poetry of Aldous Huxley*, Chatto and Windus, to the Estate of Aldous Huxley and the publishers; for Elizabeth Jennings's 'After a Play' from *Collected Poems*, Carcanet Press (1988), and 'Essentials to Shakespeare' from *Shakespeare's Company*, Celandine Press (1985), to the author and publishers; for Michael Longley's 'Fleance' from *Poems 1963–1983*, Secker and Warburg (1991), to the author; for Julie Lumsden's 'Walk Ons', to the author; for Louis MacNeice's 'Death of an Actress' from *Collected Poems*, Faber and Faber (1949), to the author's estate and the publishers; for John Masefield's 'For G B S Ninety', published in *G B S Ninety*, Hutchinson (1946), to the Society of Authors as the literary representative of the Estate of John Masefield; for Derwent May's 'A Midsummer Night's Dream in Regent's Park', published in *Messages*, edited by Naomi Lewis, Faber and Faber (1985), to the author; for Edwin Morgan's 'Instructions to an Actor' from *Collected Poems*, Carcanet Press, reprinted in *An Anthology of Poetry for Shakespeare*, selected by Charles Osborne, Bishopsgate Press (1988), to the author and Carcanet Press Ltd; for Charles Osborne's 'The Aged Actor Speaks' from *Letter to W H Auden and Other Poems, 1941–1984*, John Calder, London, and Riverrun Press, New York (1984), to the author; for Katie Parker's 'The Actor', to the author; for Eden Phillpotts's 'Theatre' from *A Hundred Sonnets*, Benn (1929), to the author's estate and A & C Black Ltd; for Carl Sandburg's 'They All Want to Play Hamlet' from *Smoke and Steel* by Carl Sandburg, copyright 1920 by Harcourt Brace Jovanovich, Inc and renewed 1948 by Carl Sandburg, to the publishers; for Louis Simpson's 'Chocolates' from *Caviare at the Funeral*, Franklin Watts, New York (1980), to the author and publishers; for Sacheverell Sitwell's 'Actor Rehearsing' from *The Thirteenth Caesar*, Grant Richards (1924), to the author's estate and the publishers; for Alison Skilbeck's 'A Sonnet', to the author; for Nicholas Smith's 'Theatre', 'The Actor Out of Work', 'Last Night', 'To the Members of the Audience' and 'Epitaph for an Actor in the Television Age', to the author; for Bryan Stocks's 'Sonnet for Shakespeare', to the author; for L A G Strong's 'A Memory' and 'An Old Woman Outside the Abbey Theatre' from *Dublin Days*, Hamish Hamilton (1923), to the Peters Fraser & Dunlop Group Ltd; for Stephen Surrey's 'American Student Actors' and 'Children Leaving a Pantomime', to the author; for May Swenson's 'To Make a Play' from *Half Sun, Half Sleep*, Scribner, New York (1967), to R R Knudson on behalf of the Literary Estate of May Swenson; for Arthur Symons's 'At the Stage Door' and 'Prologue' from *London Nights*, Leonard Smithers (1895), to A & C Black Ltd; for A S J Tessimond's 'Chaplin' from *The Collected Poems of A S J Tessimond*, White Knights Press, to Hubert Nicholson, the poet's literary executor and editor; for Anna Thomas's 'Why Do We Do It?', to the author; for Anthony Thwaite's 'The Play's the Thing' from *Poems 1953–1988*, Hutchinson (1989), to the author; for John Updike's 'Mime' from *Tossing and Turning* by John Updike, Deutsch (1977), copyright © 1977 by John Updike, to Alfred A Knopf, Inc and Andre Deutsch Ltd; for Hugo Williams's 'Going Round Afterwards', © Hugo

ACKNOWLEDGEMENTS

Williams 1985, from *Writing Home* by Hugo Williams (1985), to Oxford University Press; for P G Wodehouse's 'Mr Beerbohm Tree' and 'The Audience at the Court' from *The Parrot and Other Poems*, Hutchinson (1985), to the author's estate and the publishers; for extracts from Donald Wolfit's 'Lines to the rhythm of a well-known poem', to Donald Wolfit's Estate; for Malcolm Wroe's 'Nothing Unusual about Today' and 'Prosaic Justice', to Patricia MacNaughton, MLR Ltd, on behalf of the author.

The editor and publisher have taken all possible care to trace the copyright of all verse reprinted in this volume, and to make acknowledgement of its use. If any errors have accidentally occurred, they will be corrected in subsequent editions, provided notification is sent to the publisher.

Index of first lines

307

Index of authors

Anonymous works are listed under title